OPPORTUNITIES IN
BANKING CAREERS

Adrian A. Paradis
Revised by
Philip A. Perry

Foreword by
Connie Landry
President
Financial Women International

VGM Career Horizons
a division of *NTC Publishing Group*
Lincolnwood, Illinois USA

Cover Photo Credits:

Front cover: upper left, Citibank; upper right, First
Chicago; lower left, Wang Labs, Inc.; lower right,
Continental Bank.

Back cover: upper left, First Chicago; upper right,
Wang Labs, Inc.; lower left, NTC print.

Library of Congress Cataloging-in-Publication Data

Paradis, Adrian A.
  Opportunities in banking careers / Adrian Paradis.

      p.   cm. — (VGM career books)
  Rev. edition
  Summary: Provides an overview of the banking industry and
information on educational requirements, employment opportunities,
salaries, and advancement possibilities in this field.
  ISBN 0-8442-4050-8 (sft bnd.) — ISBN 0-8442-4049-4 (hrd bnd.)
  1. Banks and banking—Vocational guidance.   2. Banks and banking—
United States—Vocational guidance.   [1. Banks and banking—
Vocational guidance.   2. Vocational guidance.]   I. Title.
II. Series.
HG1573.P37   1993
332.1′023′73—dc20   92–44175
                                                                  CIP
                                                                   AC

Published by VGM Career Horizons, a division of NTC Publishing Group.
© 1993 by NTC Publishing Group, 4255 West Touhy Avenue,
Lincolnwood (Chicago), Illinois 60646-1975 U.S.A.

ABOUT THE AUTHORS

Adrian A. Paradis was born in Brooklyn, New York, and graduated from Dartmouth College and Columbia University's School of Library Service. As a writer, businessman, vocational specialist, and researcher, he has published widely with more than fifty titles to his credit. He has covered subjects that range from banking to biographies of contemporary businessmen and scientists; from public relations to religion; from vocational guidance to reference works; and from economics to law. In addition, he has worked on reports and special studies in his capacity as a corporate executive.

Mr. Paradis spent over twenty years as an officer of a major national corporation handling corporate matters, economic analysis, stockholder relations, corporate philanthropic contributions, and security and general administrative responsibilities. He and his wife Grace live in Sugar Hill, New Hampshire, where he serves as editor of Phoenix Publishing, a small firm which specializes in regional trade books and New England town histories.

Philip A. Perry prepared the 1992 revised edition. He is an independent editor based in Evanston, Illinois. He has worked for national business magazines and specialized in reporting on business and the economy. He was associate editor of *Real Estate Today* for five years, covering real estate finance.

PREFACE

It was Friday, March 3, 1933, the day before Franklin Delano Roosevelt was inaugurated as President of the United States.

A young man bolted his lunch and rushed to the bank to deposit his paycheck. He handed the deposit slip and check to the teller who glanced about him nervously and then leaned forward and whispered: "If I were you I'd just cash that check—don't deposit it. I just heard that every bank in the country is going to close tonight."

The young man's eyes widened. "Give it to me in fives," he said. Too frightened to count the bills he received, he fled from the bank.

This was a black day indeed. There was scarcely a state in which some banks were not closed or partially closed. Numerous offices and factories were idle. Twelve million or more people were said to be without jobs. Forlorn men stood on street corners of large cities trying to sell apples to people who could afford to buy them. Grim humorists in New York City were advising those who planned to visit the Wall Street area to take their umbrellas with them. Every few minutes a banker jumped out of a window. The nation was in the grip of terror.

"There is nothing to fear but fear itself," President Roosevelt said the next day in his inauguration speech, as he tried to reassure the nation. One of his first acts was to close every bank in the country and place an embargo on the export of gold.

When the nation awoke on Monday morning, for the first time in its history every banking institution was closed. It was a weird, chilling sensation, a new experience to live without a single banking service available, to know you could not get even a penny from your bank—a penny of *your* money! Suddenly everyone realized how dependent on banks they had become.

Every savings bank throughout the United States had closed, frustrating many frugal savers who thought that they had protected themselves against such a catastrophe. At the same time many banks told depositors that they would have to give the bank sixty days' advance notice before they could withdraw money from their accounts after the banks reopened.

By Wednesday, March 8, cash became more scarce, and the bank holiday was extended. Many cities and states began to issue paper scrip to be used in place of cash until the banks reopened.

Some businesses still accepted checks. "Live and dine on your checkbook," Manhattan's Commodore and Biltmore hotels advertised. Franklin Simon, a Fifth Avenue department store, invited new charge accounts and said they would take checks in payment of bills.

Thursday, Friday, and Saturday passed and the bank holiday continued as government officials labored long hours to decide which banks were sound enough to reopen. Then Sunday evening at ten o'clock, Washington time, the President gave the first of his famous radio fireside chats.

"I do not promise you that every bank will be reopened or that individual losses will not be suffered," he declared, "but there will be no losses that possibly could be avoided; and there would have been more and greater losses had we continued to operate."

The next day when many banks reopened, confidence was restored. People poured money into the banks and an almost audible sigh of relief could be heard in every city and town as the banking crisis ended.

Much has changed since 1933. Some sweeping changes have reshaped American banking during the last few years, and it is a challenging and exciting time to enter the field. New trends like interstate branching may soon change the map of American banking.

One thing that has not changed is the need for talented people in a field like banking. As this book explains, banking has always had a key role in U.S. history. Today, U.S. bankers provide the capital for further growth here and abroad.

Banking needs people with all kinds of skills and training. High school graduates may begin as tellers, continuing their education and advancing into management. College is usually required for entry into a management trainee program, but banks will give tuition assistance to promising employees. In the ranks of senior executives, highly trained people with advanced degrees in finance, accounting, computer science, and economics are also needed.

Since the last edition was published, investment banking has gained a reputation for power and influence, and those who participated in the mergers and acquisitions of the period made business history. Investment bankers underwrote companies like Apple and Microsoft that have become icons of our high-tech business success.

Also during the latter half of the 1980s, the federal banks stabilized real estate finance during a crisis that affected many thrift institutions. The banks, federal agencies, and government sponsored corporations that serve the housing industry hold many opportunities described in this book.

Students will be reading much in the newspapers about changes, shakeouts, and downsizing. By the estimate of the American Bankers Association, the number of professional bankers grew to 1,477,600 in 1992, up from 1,362,111 in 1979. Although not as high as the 1991 total of 1,499,868, this number still represents a huge industry. By way of comparison, the steel and auto industries together employed about 1.5 million workers during the 1980s.

No one book can give a complete picture of a business as wide ranging as banking, so the reader should also consult other books, such as *Opportunities in Financial Careers,* by Michael Sumichrast and

Dean Crist, also in this series. High school students may also want to read such books as Rachel Epstein's *Investment Banking* in the Basic Investor's Library series edited by Paul Samuelson; *Banking and Finance Careers,* by Jo Ann Whatley; or *A Teenager's Guide to Money, Banking and Finance,* by David Spiselman. College-level readers may want to look into textbooks on money and banking or a more advanced work such as *Commercial Banking in an Era of Deregulation,* by Emmanuel N. Roussakis, to understand some of the recent changes in banking and banking law.

Editor's note: Some of the descriptions of individual bankers are fictionalized composite portraits, not actual individuals. They are based on the original author's research.

FOREWORD

The banking industry offers more opportunities today than ever before for those seeking an exciting, challenging career path.

Stimulated by changes in a dynamic economy, and by deregulation, financial service institutions are redefining themselves and developing innovative ways to best serve their customers.

As businesses become more competitive and more sophisticated in their financing, as tax laws and record keeping become more complex, and as consumers become more knowledgeable and more demanding in the services provided them, banking institutions will continue to identify, train, and advance articulate, intelligent, enterprising careerists.

Opportunities exist now, and new horizons will continue to open for the foreseeable future. Those who succeed will be men and women who take control of their careers, set goals, and plan to achieve them, who are willing to take calculated risks and not just play it safe. The entrepreneur is and will be valued in the banking industry of the 1990s and beyond.

The industry also provides excellent opportunities for women, who now make up forty percent of the officers and managers of the nation's banks. Women more and more are moving out of operations, human resources, and data processing—in which they are still strong—into sales and line positions with bottom line responsibilities.

For women and men, the future belongs to those who are willing to educate themselves, manage their careers, and identify and seize opportunities. It is an exciting, dynamic industry which is going to provide increasingly rewarding careers for the future.

Connie Landry, President
Financial Women
International

CONTENTS

CHAPTER 1

BANKING TODAY

A New York City resident, Elaine Manning, picked up the phone in her apartment, dialed the number of her bank and when the call was answered said: "This is nine-four-six-dash-eight-two-seven calling; identification number zero-two-nine-two-four, paying eight-six three-dash-seven, sixty-two dollars and forty cents, and one-four nine-dash-two, ten dollars and fifty cents. Thank you."

A friend who happened to walk into the room and heard what she said was confused. "Whatever did all that gibberish mean?" she asked.

Elaine smiled as she swung around to face her guest.

"I was just paying the grocery bill and the cleaners," she said. Then she explained that she had called her bank, first given the number of her bank account, then her own secret personal identification number, and followed that with the code numbers of the grocery store and the cleaners together with the amount of money she wanted transferred from her account to theirs, so that she could pay her monthly bills.

"It's so much easier than writing checks and having to do all the bookkeeping," she concluded, "but a friend of mine who has a touch tone telephone—the kind with push buttons instead of a dial—doesn't even have to talk. She does it by tapping out the numbers and there's no human contact at all!"

1

When people think of banks they hardly think of this kind of service, but it is typical of the many innovative ways banks are helping their customers. From coast to coast alert managers are seeking more attractive and easier ways for people to handle their finances.

THE EVOLUTION OF BANKING

The sophisticated banking establishment of the 1990s, with its innumerable customer services, computerized operations, branches, and far-flung business activities presents a striking contrast to those ancient banks that developed after people adopted copper, silver, and gold coins as their money or medium of exchange.

Actually banking is as old as civilization itself. The Babylonians developed a complex system of lending, borrowing, and holding money on deposit long before 2500 B.C. Later, in Greece, the shrines at Delphi, Delos, and Ephesus served as some of that country's earliest banks. Surely, the early Greeks reasoned, no one would incur the wrath of the gods by stealing money left inside the temple.

A state bank at Troy attracted capital by paying as much as 10 percent interest while an Egyptian banker invited deposits on which he paid interest and permitted the depositors to withdraw their money at will. The Romans copied the Greek banks but went even further—offering services for transferring accounts, making loans, writing checks to withdraw funds, and various other conveniences. With the fall of Rome, however, the Empire's large-scale financial dealings ceased, and during the Early Middle Ages the banking business slumped in most of Europe although it continued in parts of Asia and North Africa.

During the thirteenth and fourteenth centuries, banks were reestablished in Italy and grew rapidly as the Italians became worldwide traders. The word *bank* originated at that time. Money changers sat behind portable benches in public squares where they displayed their coins. The word *banco* (bench) symbolized the business and was carried over into the Italian word *banca* and the French noun *banque*.

With the revival of trade between Italy (and especially Venice) and other parts of the world, banks sprang up elsewhere and intricate banking systems soon evolved. Prior to this century, family and national banks played an important though little known role in Europe's growth.

The first colonists in America had little need for banks. These settlers were self-sufficient for the most part and since agriculture was the principal business, barter rather than cash served their needs at first. The original banks, called "land banks," lent money or issued bank notes to farmers who put up their property as collateral. The government of South Carolina authorized a land bank in 1712 and two years later Massachusetts did the same. Similar banks appeared shortly thereafter in all the colonies so that there would be cash to circulate among the people as well as money to finance military defenses and expeditions.

The King of England in 1741 declared the banks illegal and the colonists had to wait forty years before the first real American bank, the Bank of North America in Philadelphia, was chartered by the Continental Congress. Other private banks were soon established as was the Bank of the United States, which Congress authorized as the fiscal agent of the new federal government.

Gradually banks grew in number, size, and importance. The financial stability of the young republic was tied to the fortunes of its banks and their ability to provide financial banking for the challenging expansion to the West. As the cities grew and their industry expanded, they too needed banking credit and services. Even as the wagon trains pushed west across the plains and over the mountains, settlement after settlement sprang up and with them the little banks so necessary for every community. New banks are still opening today while many of the older ones are merging or being acquired by foreigners. What's more, the industry is more dynamic than ever—adjusting to change, seeking new horizons, and becoming one of the most important elements in the lives of most citizens because banking, although it involves finance, is predominantly concerned with people.

BANKING IS PEOPLE

Banking is people—people like you, your relatives, and your friends. Banking is people dedicated to performing a variety of financial services for others to help make their lives happier, easier, and more productive. Banking is not the typical fortresslike granite structure in the country village or the soaring stainless steel and glass tower rising from the city street. Behind the façade you find people, thousands and thousands of men and women who are performing a tremendous variety of jobs, most of whom are proud of their responsibilities, eager to please the public they serve, and eager for promotions to more challenging and better paying positions.

Since you are interested in learning about this business, the rewards it may offer, and how you might tailor your talents to it, in the chapters that follow we will sketch the romance of banking, suggest what it is like today to work in a bank, and show the multitude of opportunities awaiting those who choose a banking career. Perhaps one of the most interesting things about banking is that regardless of your interest or skills, the industry is almost certain to have a place for you.

Banking is not just receiving and paying out money at a teller's window—the only part of banking that most people ever see. Banking is high finance—lending money to distant kings and small grocers alike; it is public relations and advertising; it is helping people buy their homes, automobiles, refrigerators, and all the other things they need or want; it is regulating the nation's economy; it is running gigantic computers that transfer huge sums of money without ever touching a dollar bill; it is counseling foreigners who barely speak English on how to manage their financial affairs; it is helping establish scholarships to enable more young Americans to attend college. It is all these things and many many more, but most of all banking is people—an honorable and useful occupation! And inasmuch as banking is people, the ways that banks operate reflect the imagination, the hard work, and the goals of the men and women connected with them.

THE MANY FACES OF BANKING

In an effort to call the bank to the attention of the public and create a pleasant, relaxing atmosphere where shoppers and businessmen could pause to relax at noontime, a large metropolitan savings bank recently began offering concerts in the lobby from noon until two o'clock. It was an experiment that proved so popular that the concerts were scheduled on a permanent basis.

"Is this banking?" some people were heard to ask as they stood listening to a piece played by a string quartet. Banks were traditionally thought of as conservative businesses that did not have to call attention to themselves. Everyone needed a bank, hence all a banker had to do was open the doors and wait for the customers to arrive.

This is no longer the case, however. As the number of banking institutions grows, the competition becomes keener and managements must become increasingly resourceful to attract and hold new business. The need to obtain large amounts of capital has spawned the great giveaway plans that are so popular in many cities, especially among money-hungry savings banks. Just for opening an account a new depositor is offered a wide choice of gifts. The larger the deposit the more valuable the gifts. Thus in one bank an initial deposit of just $250 could earn you a tote bag, a spice rack, a lamp, or a folding chair, whereas $5,000 would give you a clock radio, a Polaroid camera, a toaster oven, or an electric coffee pot. This is better than buying sweepstake tickets or betting on horses—your money is in a safe place, you have your prize, and you are earning interest besides.

"Who Will Give You $50 For $45?" read the caption headline under a picture showing a crowd of elderly people lined up before a bank. The answer was that the Sterling National Bank and Trust Company would if you were over fifty and one of the first one hundred people waiting outside the bank's main office. The giveaway helped celebrate the bank's fiftieth anniversary.

Meanwhile, a rural bank in New Hampshire advertised: "Señor Citizens: Señora Citizens: Señorita Citizens: We do more for you! Sí! Now! New! Bill-Payer Service. No charge! You're our guest; Let us pay your monthly bill; You give us your authorization; Have your Social Security check deposited directly; Plus you get top interest on your account; Sí! Sign up now, not mañana!"

Publicity and Advertising for the Banking Industry

This kind of publicity and advertising is not typical of all banks; most advertising is dignified because the majority of bankers want to create the impression that their institutions are not fly-by-night or frivolous places to do business. One problem bankers have had ever since the first bank opened a few thousand years ago is that many are very wealthy individuals. Because cartoonists have long depicted bankers as portly, well-dressed men, banks still have an image problem and want people to think well of them. That is why their public relations programs are so important.

"What is public relations?" you might ask. Simply stated we might say that public relations is dealing successfully with people, with the emphasis on an activity that is beneficial to the public or that endeavors to gain the good will and understanding of the public. Providing concerts in a lobby, giving away money, or advertising a bill-payer service are examples of publicity—calling attention to oneself—not public relations.

Banks are creating good public relations when they support nonprofit public broadcasting or television, help provide certain community services in poor neighborhoods, contribute to college scholarship programs, encourage their employees to work for charities, or undertake a host of other unselfish programs all designed to gain good will or the understanding of the public. The ways that banks do this are limited only by the imagination of those who are responsible for such programs.

Competition and Innovation

Competition, attracting new capital, creating a good image, finding new customers, providing excellent service, maintaining good employee relations—these are only a few of the problems that every bank must face and that make banking such a fascinating and challenging business. A number of innovations are appearing that promise to bring changes in the business as well as exciting new opportunities for those seeking a banking career.

- Some banks are beginning to sell merchandise through catalogs to compete with Sears and other retailers that have become competitive with an increasingly wide range of financial services.
- Home banking is becoming popular with customers who have computer terminals and can use them to review the status of their accounts, pay most of their bills, switch money from one account to another, and communicate with the bank.
- Banks offer various computer services to outside businesses.
- Interstate banking will spread throughout the country as banks look for expansion opportunities.
- Global finance is a reality; electronic transfers of funds occur daily across international boundaries—multinational business requires multinational banking.
- Banks are buying established savings and loan, credit, and insurance operations to expand their services.
- Some banks are acting as discount stock brokers, selling and buying securities for their customers.

- Chemical Bank in New York City sends "Banking a la Carte" mobile teller stations into large business offices. Employees can do all their banking at the teller station.
- Some banks are sending specially trained employees out to solicit new business, as well as call on regular customers in their homes and service their accounts right in their living rooms.
- Savings and loan associations and savings banks that used to invest most of their deposits in mortgages are seeking more lucrative investments for their funds.
- Larger banks are selling services to smaller institutions.
- Numerous banks are expanding their "private banking" services for wealthy customers who keep large balances. These preferred customers receive tax, investment, and estate planning help; have access to private offices and senior officers; can use special telephone lines; and enjoy other privileges.

Banking is indeed on the march, open to new ideas, and seeking people who can accept the challenge of change!

BANKS AND FOREIGN POLICY

If the competition of foreign banks in the United States is worrisome to bank officers, there is an even more nettlesome problem that American banks are discovering as they make loans to foreign governments. Some of our large commercial banks have been providing the major portion of money needed by many overseas nations, but this business has serious implications. When these loans are not repaid on time they become disguised as financial aid to those countries, and in the eyes of the United States government the American bankers are indirectly making foreign policy decisions, thus diminishing our government's role in this field.

The ability of foreign countries to repay their loans usually depends on how much they can sell and export to the United States. This means that these nations must lobby for more favorable treatment so their exports can come into this country and these requests must be considered in order to protect the safety of our nation's banking system. Thus when American banks decide to extend more loans to a foreign government, they are taking on the character of making foreign policy decisions.

Although these are not matters that will concern the new banking employee, they nevertheless show how important our larger banks have become on the international scene and suggest some of the challenging positions experienced employees may find in those departments which handle the overseas loan business.

International intrigue, however, is an intangible aspect of banking as far as jobs are concerned and offers few career opportunities. Instead, your future might lie with the Federal Reserve or one of the several government-sponsored banks. But it will probably start with the familiar commercial or savings bank, or perhaps with a credit union, a cooperative bank, or a consumer loan or mortgage banking office, depending on your special interests and skills as well as available job opportunities. There are approximately forty-eight thousand commercial or full-service banks in the United States, ranging from fewer than ten employees to over ten thousand in metropolitan areas. Many of these banks operate one or more branches in addition to their main offices. Before we examine each of these institutions, perhaps it would be useful to familiarize ourselves with a typical commercial bank.

CHAPTER 2

BANKERS AT WORK

What is your definition of a *bank*? You probably visualize a large room with a counter along one side behind which stand tellers who receive and pay out money. At one end of the banking floor you may see a number of men and women sitting at large, highly polished desks. Generally these employees have the most dealings with the bank's customers. They may be responsible for opening new accounts, discussing loan applications, handling all the paperwork required for considering and granting mortgages, explaining the bank's possible role in setting up a trust, and arranging for the rental of a safe deposit box. At the far end of the banking lobby, opposite those employees seated at the desks, might be a huge steel door that opens to the safe deposit vault where customers may rent individual lock boxes to store valuable papers, jewelry, and other items.

This is what the word *bank* means to many of us, but like the tip of the iceberg, there is much more to it than you may think. For example, the quick and efficient way that the tellers handle each transaction is possible only because there are scores of people working behind the scenes. Every time a customer hands a deposit to a teller, that transaction must be recorded on the customer's account as well as on the bank's own accounting records. Similarly, whenever a teller counts out those crisp green bills and gives them to the customer who is cashing a check or withdrawing funds, another entry must be made on the customer's account as well as on the bank's books. These entries reflect the changes in both the customer's and the bank's cash positions. Multiply these deposit and withdrawal transactions by the hundreds or thousands of customers who come to the bank and its branches each day, and you realize the enormity of the task and why it calls for many other employees whom the public never sees.

Likewise, there is much more involved than meets the eye when a customer applies for a loan of $300 or for a $100,000 mortgage. The bank's lending officer must first research the customer's reliability and financial condition before deciding whether it would be safe to lend the money. Once a mortgage is granted, systems must be set up to make certain the regular monthly payments, taxes, and insurance are paid on time. In the case of banks that specialize in making thousands of small loans, imagine the tremendous amount of behind-the-scenes activity!

FULL-SERVICE BANKING

Consider for a moment some of the other services that banks offer their customers, many of which require a separate department or group of employees. *Full-service* is an enticing phrase that some smart banker invented and which the gasoline stations copied. Today the public takes a full-service bank for granted, but just what full service really means we leave to your imagination. Probably it is what many banks have been offering as normal services for years. At any rate, these are some of the principal services banks make available to their customers.

Special Savings Accounts

In addition to regular savings accounts, Christmas and vacation clubs are featured widely. These are specialized savings accounts that force savers to make regular weekly deposits so they will have a certain sum of money available to buy Christmas presents or to take a vacation at the end of a twelve-month period.

"But can't people save without having to bother the bank to institute this type of special savings account?" you may well ask. The answer is "yes," except that most people will not discipline themselves and the banks are delighted to have the extra business.

Direct Deposits

Men and women who receive Social Security or pension checks may have the funds sent directly to their bank to be deposited to their accounts. In areas where thieves often steal these checks from mailboxes and illegally cash them, this is a very valuable service for which banks do not charge.

Traveler's Checks

People going abroad who need to carry large sums of money need not take cash. Instead they can buy traveler's checks inexpensively at the bank. These checks usually come in denominations of $10, $25, $50 or $100 and can be cashed anywhere in the world. If you lose your checks all you do is notify the bank and replacements are issued. What could be safer or easier?

Bank Cards

In this day of credit cards, banks have not overlooked this important convenience. Most banks offer their customers one of two cards: *Master Card* or *Visa*. The customer can charge any thing offered for sale wherever the card symbol is displayed and billed monthly by the bank for all the items purchased. An annual fee is charged to the customer for this service. Also, the store or restaurant pays the bank a small percentage of the amount charged. If the cardholder remits only a portion of the amount due, the banks charge interest on the balance—another convenient way for the customer to obtain credit!

As we have already seen, what could be easier than to pick up the telephone, dial the bank and tell the voice at the other end to pay your telephone and grocery bills? Along the same line, many banks are installing systems whereby you can go to the grocery store and use a plastic credit card to pay for your groceries. The store sends the cash register slip to the bank which transfers funds from your account to the store's. A painless way to shop indeed!

International Services

A tiny old woman limped into a large city bank and went up to the nearest teller. "Please, I should like to send some money to my daughter in Poland?"

The teller smiled and quickly made arrangements so that a few days later the woman received the Polish banknotes that she then mailed to her daughter.

In the same bank a businesswoman approached one of the officers.

"I have to send five hundred thousand dollars to a French manufacturer," she said. "Can you help me?"

"Of course," the officer replied, opening a drawer and reaching for a printed form. Within an hour $500,000 had been transferred to a Paris bank which notified the nearby company that the money had been deposited to its account.

Financing

The same bank officer was later approached by a businessman who needed advice about financing a new addition for his plant. They spent over two hours discussing the project and when the grateful businessman left he knew his plan for expansion was impractical and the bank had saved him from making what surely would have turned out to be a costly mistake.

Trust Departments

Every time someone buys or sells stock on one of the nation's stock exchanges the stock must be transferred to another name and the new ownership registered. Who does this? In most cases the corporate trust departments of banks. In addition they may also send out all the dividend checks, annual and quarterly reports, and special mailings and answer countless letters from stockholders.

Another important banking service is designated by the conservative lettering on the glass door that reads "Trust Department." Here a large group of employees is busy taking care of the financial affairs of people who want the bank to manage their money. These department members also handle all the details involved in settling estates for those who have arranged to have the bank act as their executor. On the other hand a customer may set up a trust which stipulates that a certain large sum of money must be managed and paid out according to very stringent terms to certain persons under certain conditions. These and other trust assignments are extremely important responsibilities, because in some cases customers may entrust millions of dollars to the judgment of the men and women who work for the bank.

Skilled Employees

By now you can see that full-service banking means just that—comprehensive services of every kind to meet every banking need a customer could possibly have. To provide this kind of service requires many employees of diverse skills and experience, This is an area of the bank you seldom see, so let's look briefly at what actually takes place behind the scenes.

BEHIND THE SCENES

Since banks come in all sizes and differ greatly in the ways they conduct their business, the departments mentioned here, though typical of those you will find in most institutions, may vary greatly with regard to their names, sizes, and functions.

Operations Department

The busiest and largest department is usually operations, for here a group of employees handles the greatest amount of paperwork, much of which is generated by the paying and receiving tellers who work on practically all the bank's transactions. As previously noted, every check received or dollar paid out starts a long flow of paperwork. Take the paycheck that Martha Green deposits as an example.

The teller receives Ms. Green's paycheck together with a deposit slip bearing her name and account number. The teller records the amount of the deposit on a special machine that issues a pink receipt to be given to her. This is not the end of the transaction, though, for Ms. Green needs some cash and so hands the teller her own personal check drawn to cash for twenty-five dollars. When Ms. Green picks up the crisp new bills and makes room for the next person in line, she has left behind a check drawn on a bank in a distant city, a deposit slip directing that her paycheck is to be deposited to her account, and her own check that has been cashed. At the end of the day the teller must balance the cash with all the deposits and withdrawals. Once this is accomplished, the teller sees that the out-of-town checks go to the transit department and that all the deposit slips and checks received go to the bookkeeping department.

Here a computer operator electronically sends the information to the computer which records the transactions on the bank's and Ms. Green's records. At the same time, the transit department employees are sorting out-of-town checks into various categories, making certain that the total of all the checks is accurately computed and correctly entered on the bank's records. Then the checks are bundled and placed in special mailing containers to go to the nearest Federal Reserve Bank.

Marketing Department

Recently many banks have organized marketing departments to "market" or sell their services to the public. Any business must constantly attract new customers and expand if it hopes to keep its doors open and prosper. Banks are no exception, and as competition increases, each institution must double its efforts to find new accounts and persuade the public that it is offering the finest and most complete service. In a small bank one of the top officers is usually responsible for carrying out the marketing program, but in large banking companies each department may be responsible for its own marketing, or there may be a marketing department to carry out the bank's sales, advertising, and public relations programs.

Maintenance

In a small bank, the custodian who empties the wastepaper baskets and mops the floors also tends the furnace and acts as a handyman when something needs repairs. Larger banks have their own maintenance departments staffed with specialists who not only handle the custodial services, but also maintain the machines, air conditioning, heating, and other mechanical apparatus. These same banks probably have a purchasing department too, because it makes sense to centralize the task of buying hundreds of items ranging from paper clips or ballpoint pens to furniture, electric adding machines, or even pickup trucks to transport files to the warehouse.

Personnel

Since banking is people who provide services for other people, the personnel department is a vital part of the enterprise. It is not only responsible for hiring employees but also for supervising all of the personnel services that the bank offers and which may be extensive—especially in a large bank with many branches. Salary administration is an area of increasing importance which assures that fair guidelines for setting salaries and governing increases are established. Employee benefit programs are widespread because many banks now offer health and life insurance, pensions, profit-sharing plans, as well as disability and unemployment compensation. Determining the bank's policy on vacations, sick pay, and time off for special purposes is also a concern of this department.

One major responsibility of the personnel department is maintaining records on all employees—no small responsibility, especially in a bank that operates in an urban area and has a large number of workers and a steady turnover. With the advent of federal "Affirmative Action" programs that encourage businesses to hire and promote more women and members of minority groups, employee management can be a challenging assignment. The Affirmative Action officer must work closely with all department heads to see what opportunities there may be for placing women and minority applicants, as well as to make certain that these people receive equal consideration with other employees for promotion.

Administration

So far no mention has been made of the men and women who administer the overall affairs of the bank. They are the officers, who range from chairman of the board down through president, vice-presidents, cashier, auditor, security manager, and assistant officers. Promotion to the position of officer is the reward for the men and women who learn the business, apply themselves, and become useful and reliable

employees. Since we are concerned primarily with beginning or intermediate positions which may eventually lead to that of officer, we shall
mention only that these experienced and capable individuals are the
people who direct the overall operations of the bank. At the same time
they are responsible for seeing to it that the bank earns a profit, which
brings us now to the all-important subject of lending.

MONEY TO LEND

When you consider the cost of running a bank—operating the various
departments that we have just described briefly, maintaining and paying
taxes on office space in the main building and branches, meeting the
payroll each week, renting the data processing machines, and buying
office furniture, to name but a few items—you cannot help but realize
that the money for these expenses must come from somewhere. But
where?

The answer is that the bulk of the bank's income comes from the
interest earned from lending money. It is true that other income is
realized from performing services in the personal and corporate trust
departments, renting safe deposit vaults, and providing other services,
but all the money realized from these activities is nothing compared to
the income realized from loans.

"Lend, lend, lend!" was what a bank president told employees when
he resolved to turn the bank into a profitable business again. Money
does little good stored up in a vault. For this reason, the commercial or
business loans that a bank makes constitute the "profit center" of that
bank. Commercial loans are made for a variety of purposes: to develop
new products, build new factories, invest in securities, lease equipment,
buy livestock for a farm, purchase property, and many others. Most
Americans are familiar with their bank's mortgage department which
lends money to home owners and thereby enables millions of families
to own their own homes. Loans to buy new automobiles and appliances,

make home improvements, acquire clothing, and all the other things we want are common too, as banks expand their consumer loan business.

In later sections of this book you will see how extensive the lending business is and the countless career opportunities it offers, but first let's consider the relationship of lending to the overall banking business.

"Where does the money come from that a bank may lend?" we asked the loan officer of a small Michigan bank. A tall thin man who was never without his pipe, he motioned us to a chair and pointed his pipe towards us.

"That's easy to answer," he said, "because most of the money which we have available to lend the public comes from what you and all the bank's other depositors have in their checking accounts. That's why this money is often referred to as 'checkbook money.' We pay you, say, 5 percent interest on the money in your checking account, and then charge someone else to whom we lend it interest rates that vary between 6 and 12 percent, or more, depending on the type of loan. The difference is the profit the bank needs to pay its bills."

He paused and lit his pipe, puffing on it for a moment, then looked up. "Do you know about the Federal Reserve requirement?" he asked.

"What's that?"

"Assume for a moment that you deposit one hundred dollars in your checking account. Federal Reserve rules may require that 15 percent, or fifteen dollars, must be put into the bank's reserve account at the Federal Reserve bank. This ensures there being enough money on hand in case a number of depositors withdraw large sums of money at one time. Now the bank is free to lend the remaining 85 percent, or eighty-five dollars. However, if the Federal Reserve decides to tighten the nation's money supply it will raise the reserve requirement, say to 25 percent. That means that instead of eighty-five dollars being available of your one-hundred dollar deposit, only seventy-five dollars may be lent. Thus the bank has fewer dollars to lend its customers." He smiled and puffed a few times, then added, "If this sounds intricate, it really isn't, especially if you deal with it every day."

"This really affects the bank's ability to lend money, doesn't it, but more than that, it must have a tremendous effect on the nation's economy."

"Definitely," he agreed, "but I daresay that the average person in the street is not aware of it."

Since the Federal Reserve seems so important, it might be useful to see how the Federal Reserve System operates and how it is tied in with the country's banking system as well as its overall economy.

CHAPTER 3

THE FEDERAL RESERVE BANK

If you were to visit our nation's capital, which attractions would you like to see? Most tourists are eager to visit the White House, the Washington Monument, the Lincoln Memorial, and the Smithsonian Institution. Few people seek out the headquarters of our country's central bank, the Federal Reserve Building on Constitution Avenue. This three-story H-shaped building constructed of white Georgia marble sits back some distance from the street, offering a fine view of its simple beauty. Window frames are of bronze, a white American eagle guards the main entrance, and wide marble hallways within lead to the various offices and meeting rooms used by the governors who head the Federal Reserve System.

The Federal Reserve Bank is the most important banking system in America, and yet it is the least understood! Although it does not offer the same career opportunities as commercial and savings institutions, there are numerous job opportunities and some unique career possibilities that enable an individual to participate personally in helping to establish national fiscal policies. The well-being of the United States often depends on the decisions of the Federal Reserve System.

EVOLUTION OF THE FEDERAL RESERVE

To understand and appreciate the importance and the various functions of the Federal Reserve banks, it is necessary to look back to the last century when the nation's 1,600 banks were issuing about 10,000 different kinds of bank notes which then served as currency. Some notes were good, some worth but half the amount printed on them, and many were worthless. Counterfeit bills were easily printed and passed freely. After a wave of bank closings caused thousands of Americans to lose their savings in 1857, businessmen and even astute bankers were unable to determine which bank notes were good and which were worthless or counterfeit. The situation became so unwieldy that in 1863 Congress passed an act creating a national currency. Thereafter national banks chartered by the government were permitted to issue paper money only if their bank notes were backed by federal bonds that had been deposited with the Treasurer of the United States. Three years later, a tax on all notes issued by state banks forced them to stop printing their own money and obtain national charters. At last the country had sound currency. But this step by itself was not enough.

Once the transcontinental railroad opened in 1869, wave after wave of immigrants headed West to settle the new frontiers. At the same time, industrialists were building new factories in the East and the Midwest, hoping to fill all the orders for goods that a growing country required. As the population and industrial activity expanded, a currency shortage gradually developed. Smaller banks in the areas distant from the big cities had difficulty obtaining enough money to satisfy the needs of their customers.

Creation of the Federal Reserve

The currency shortage had become so severe by 1907 that Congress appointed the National Monetary Commission to study the problem and recommend a solution. The Commission discovered that countries whose currency supply could expand or contract to meet the needs of business usually had some kind of central bank that could issue currency as needed. The Federal Reserve Act of 1913 was the result of Congress listening to the pleas of people living in the South and West, far removed from the nation's capital and from New York City, the nation's financial hub. Instead of depending on one central bank, like the Bank of England, a decentralized Federal Reserve System was created consisting of twelve Federal Reserve banks located in Boston, New York, Philadelphia, Cleveland, Richmond, Atlanta, Chicago, St. Louis, Minneapolis, Kansas City, Dallas, and San Francisco. Each bank served a particular Federal Reserve district. More than 40 percent of the nation's banks, which hold 75 percent of the country's bank deposits, are now members of the Federal Reserve System. Under this arrangement America's economic and financial policies would be set by bankers who represented every part of the country, instead of only officials and bankers in New York and Washington.

The basic purpose of the Federal Reserve is to make possible a flow of credit and money that will assure orderly economic growth and a stable dollar. The system is like the adrenal glands in our bodies. When we need extra energy to meet an emergency the glands release hormones into the blood stream. When our economy is in trouble and more money and credit are needed, the Federal Reserve System releases them. Conversely, when it appears that the nation is on an inflationary course because there is too much money, the system tightens the credit reins and thus retards economic activity.

Managing the Nation's Money Supply

FED ACTS TO REDUCE RATES (By Dave Skidmore, Associated Press) WASHINGTON—The Federal Reserve added money to the nation's banking system today in a move many economists took as a clear signal that the central bank was lowering interest rates.

Many economists said they believe the Federal Reserve lowered the target for the federal funds rate—the rate banks charge one another on overnight loans—by a quarter of a percentage point to 3 percent.

Economists said the first priority of the Federal Reserve is the domestic economy, which has been struggling for two years now to shake off the effects of the recession.

(source: Chicago *Sun-Times,* Friday, Sept. 4, 1992. Final Markets
. edition p. 8, final markets wrap.)

It's all well and good that we're told what the Federal Reserve intends to do to manage the nation's money supply, but how does it accomplish this? There are three principal ways, and you will see them reported in your newspaper from time to time.

The first is by raising or lowering the "discount rate," which is the amount of interest banks have to pay the Federal Reserve when they borrow money. The banks, in turn, then raise or lower the interest rates they charge their customers who need money. This has the effect of making it either harder or easier for business to borrow money.

The second way the Federal Reserve regulates our money supply is by raising or lowering the "reserve requirements" of member banks. As noted in the previous chapter this is the method of increasing or decreasing the amount of your "checkbook money," because as banks are required to put more or less of their funds into their reserve accounts, the amount of money available to lend is affected.

The third way is through the Federal Reserve's "open market operations." Every three or four weeks the Federal Open Market Committee meets in the Federal Reserve building in Washington. It consists of the governors, the presidents of the twelve Federal Reserve Banks, and top staff members who determine the Federal Reserve system's policies for the weeks ahead. The decisions that the group reach will affect not only the economy of this country but also foreign trade and possibly international financial transactions. If it is decided that money and credit should be loosened, the New York Federal Reserve Bank's six securities traders will be instructed to buy huge blocks of United States Treasury notes. Millions of dollars then flow into the banks as they sell the securities they are holding. Thus the banks have more money to lend their customers.

RESPONSIBILITIES OF THE FEDERAL RESERVE

Because it performs several vital services for the nation's commercial banks the Federal Reserve has been called the banker's bank. As mentioned before, it decides the amount of reserves a bank must keep and provides banks with currency and coin, as well as short-term loans. One of the most extensive services it provides involves clearing out checks. Every day Americans write millions of checks that go to all parts of the country in payment for goods and services. When a merchant in Los Angeles receives a check drawn on a bank in Richmond, Virginia, there must be a mechanism whereby the check is returned to the account of the drawer and the money transferred to Los Angeles. This miracle is performed many times daily—much of it by computer—with no hitches or problems. Thus, the Federal Reserve keeps the wheels of the nation's commerce turning.

The Federal Reserve also acts as the fiscal agent and bank for the federal government, buying and selling its treasury bills. This in itself is a huge job, inasmuch as the government runs a multibillion dollar operation! Additionally the Federal Reserve also regulates and super-vises all the activities of its member banks throughout the nation. As we shall see later, this is done by each of the individual twelve Federal Reserve banks.

CAREER OPPORTUNITIES IN WASHINGTON, D.C.

Research activities of the Federal Reserve Board are conducted in academic-like surroundings by groups of economic experts in the Divisions of Research and Statistics and International Finance. The highly skilled economists are supported by a strong junior professional staff, economic editing services, and one of the country's leading economic and financial reference libraries. This research staff is recognized the world over for its contributions to economic and monetary knowledge.

The Board works closely with each of the twelve Federal Reserve Banks and their branches through its three divisions: Federal Reserve Bank Operations, Banking Supervision and Regulation, and Consumer and Community Affairs. The Legal Division provides council to the Board on questions and problems that arise in commercial, corporate, antitrust, administrative, and banking law.

The Data Processing Division supports the Board in research, administration, and policy areas by providing computer services, analysis and information. The division has earned an outstanding reputation for leadership in applying computer technology to the processing and presentation of economic gain.

Opportunities are available at the Federal Reserve Board for economists, economic research assistants, financial analysts, examiners, attorneys, applications programmers, and systems analysts. In addition, other opportunities exist for clerical and support positions.

The Board offers an extensive benefits package which includes annual vacation and sick leave; life, health, and dental insurance; and an attractive savings plan that offers tax deferral options. For more information about career opportunities, write to Human Resource Management, Board of Governors of the Federal Reserve System, 21st and Constitution Avenue, N.W., Washington, DC 20551.

CAREERS IN THE FIELD

Located in the downtown section of Kansas City, Missouri, in a modern, twenty-story building where approximately 900 people are employed is one of the smaller Federal Reserve Banks. In addition another 800 employees work in the three branch offices in Denver,

Oklahoma City, and Omaha, which serve the local needs for certain banking services. Like each of the other eleven Federal Reserve Banks, this bank is a corporation whose capital stock is owned by member banks within its district. However, the power to regulate and control its activities is vested in the Board of Governors of the Federal Reserve System, and ultimately in Congress.

Mature college graduates whose personal development is enhanced by in-bank training may assume ever-increasing job responsibilities at this bank. Many graduates who have been with the bank five years or less hold highly responsible management positions. They are good examples of the rapid promotional opportunities offered by this bank.

Initially you are assigned to one of several important areas within the bank, depending on your interests, qualifications, and the bank's current personnel needs. If you aspire to one of these positions, you should have a degree in fields related to business administration, computer science, mathematics, or other applicable areas of the sciences and liberal arts.

These are the principal departments which seek new employees from time to time:

The Internal Auditing Department reviews all the operations of the bank itself. As an auditor you would review procedures for conformity with established security controls, bank policies, Federal Reserve System regulations, and federal and local laws. Discrepancies and recommendations for correcting them are summarized in writing upon the completion of an audit. Limited travel is required in this position and graduates with a basic knowledge of accounting and auditing are considered for openings.

The Computer Systems Department is involved in systems and software design and applications programming related to the information and processing needs of all departments within the bank. In other words, this department is responsible for operating the computers that provide rapid access to various data bases at each district office. In addition, major commercial member banks have direct telecommunications to the bank through the computers. A person with a degree in computer science or equivalent work experience would find this a challenging career.

The Personnel Department administers continuing programs in employment and wage and salary administration, including performance reviews and labor market surveys. Personnel analysts also help manage employee benefits and training programs for the bank. The department also formulates and administers personnel policies for the bank and branch personnel. Here too, a well-rounded education and/or related work experience are desirable.

The Accounting Department maintains the general ledger books of the Federal Reserve Bank of Kansas City. In addition, departmental staff members maintain reserve and discount loan accounts for commercial banks in the district and treasury accounts are maintained for the federal government. A nationwide communications system makes possible payments and transfers of money between financial institutions on a daily basis. Accounting analysts compile data and prepare written reports analyzing these financial activities and recommend improvements or modifications in departmental operations. Graduates with an accounting degree or related experience are welcomed here.

The Financial Control Department prepares the bank's budget and monitors all expenditures. It also performs cost analysis studies. Opportunities are afforded in this work for a college graduate's professional development.

The Check Collection Department clears and processes all checks for the commercial banks in the area. A computerized accounting system enables reserve accounts to be adjusted rapidly as money in the form of checks flows between commercial banks. Transportation methods must be improved continually to provide more efficient service to the banks.

The Bank Supervision and Structure Division supervises and regulates member bank activities and supervises the formation of bank holding companies as well as their operation and expansion.

The Bank Holding Company Supervision Departments examine member banks for compliance with banking regulations, Federal Reserve regulations, and state banking laws. College graduates with twelve or more hours of college accounting or related experience who enjoy extensive travel would find bank examination an interesting career.

The Research Division encompasses both economic research and public affairs activities. Economists conduct research studies dealing with the entire range of economic and financial considerations that must be taken into account in forming monetary policy. This work includes analyzing and appraising national economic developments, regional trends, and international aspects. The results of many of these studies are published in periodicals or special booklets. Its public affairs department (usually called public relations in industry) coordinates press relations for the bank as a whole and works closely with the various news media. The department also maintains the Economic Research Library. Graduates with degrees in economics, mathematics, statistics, library science, or journalism will find entry level jobs while doctoral degrees are a prerequisite for senior staff positions in economic research.

In addition to all of these departmental specialist positions, the bank employs numerous clerical, secretarial, and other office personnel. The bank has a policy of internal promotions and a sound salary administration program based on performance, while at the same time offering a wide range of employee benefits that compare most favorably with those offered by large industrial corporations.

The following personnel policy of the Federal Reserve Bank of Kansas City might be said to be typical of most of the Federal Reserve Banks:

> It is the policy of the Federal Reserve Bank of Kansas City to provide an environment of equal employment opportunity. The Bank attempts to utilize the best available talent without regard to race, color, religion, sex, age or national origin. Opportunities are

provided for each employee to develop the skills needed for maximum achievement and advancement. Emphasis is placed upon the
recruitment and utilization of minority group members, women,
and handicapped persons in order to insure equal employment
opportunity at all levels and in all areas of the Bank.

As a matter of operating policy, each Federal Reserve Bank is auton-
omous in that it carries out its own manpower planning activities and
employment program. Since the personnel requirements of the individual banks change frequently, you should apply directly to the Personnel
Officer of the bank listed below which interests you.

BOSTON
600 Atlantic Avenue
Boston, MA 02106

NEW YORK
33 Liberty Street
Federal Reserve P.O. Station
New York, NY 10045

PHILADELPHIA
10 Independence Mall
Philadelphia, PA 19105

CLEVELAND
1455 East Sixth Street
P.O. Box 6386
Cleveland, OH 44101

RICHMOND
701 E. Byrd Street
P.O. Box 27622
Richmond, VA 23261

ATLANTA
104 Marietta Street, N.W.
Atlanta, GA 30303

CHICAGO
230 South LaSalle Street
P.O.Box 834
Chicago, IL 60690

ST. LOUIS
411 Locust Street
P.O. Box 442
St. Louis, MO 63166

MINNEAPOLIS
250 Marquette Avenue
Minneapolis, MN 55480

KANSAS CITY
925 Grand Avenue
Federal Reserve Station
Kansas City, MO 64198

DALLAS
2200 N. Pearl
Station K
Dallas, TX 75222

SAN FRANCISCO
400 Sansome Street
P.O. Box 7702
San Francisco, CA 94120

Later we will discuss many of the interesting banking positions—their responsibilities and opportunities—in detail. First, however, it would seem wise to take an overall look at the different types of banks and financial institutions and see what makes banking so exciting, different, and challenging for those seeking careers in this growing field.

CHAPTER 4

COMMERCIAL BANKING

BIRTH OF A BANK

Mary Woodman was a young woman of twenty in 1901. She traveled to Solomonville, Arizona, registered at the desert town's only hotel, and found her room had no key. She lost no time going down to the lobby.

"Nobody in town uses keys," the manager explained. His statement was not reassuring, but Mary decided that she would have to learn to accept the ways of the frontier.

Solomonville, located in southeastern Arizona, was an important supply post for mining camps. The town had no bank until A.G. Smith, formerly with a large Denver bank, proposed the idea to I.E. Solomon, who had founded the town. Solomon was enthusiastic and the Gila Valley Bank opened in a corner of the general store. It was such a success that the directors decided to expand and open a branch in the small town of Clifton. It was agreed that Smith would be the manager and Mary Woodman was hired as the bookkeeper.

Her first assignment as the only other member of the branch staff was to help transport $800 in "cartwheel" silver dollars, gold fives, tens, and twenties. Most of this coin was placed in small cloth bags and sewn under her voluminous skirts. The balance of $200 was carried by three men to divert suspicion from Mary in case the party were attacked and robbed. The buckboard wound along primitive dirt roads, passed spots famous for hold-ups, and rolled into Clifton with its human cargo, gold, and silver intact. Thus, the bank's first woman employee helped to found and open its number one branch.

To complete the story, Mary Woodman later became manager of the Clifton office and the bank's first woman officer.

In 1922 the Gila Valley Bank merged with the Valley National Bank in Phoenix. Ten years later, when the country was in the throes of the Great Depression, half the employees were laid off, and assets were tied up in ranches that the bank had been forced to take over and manage. Everyone was wondering whether the bank could survive. In desperation, the directors looked for and found a new president to revive the bank: Walter Reed Bimson, a vice-president of Chicago's Harris Trust & Savings Bank. Leaving one of the largest banks in the nation, he accepted the challenge of trying to rescue a small country bank that ranked 557th in size among institutions in the United States.

Bimson's solution to the bank's problem now seems obvious, for it is the secret of later banking success. "Make loans!" he insisted. "That is the way to recovery and I want this period of automatic loan refusal to end and end now! Make loans! The biggest service we can perform today is to put money into people's hands. Let us especially go into mass production on small loans. People at this very moment need to borrow for all kinds of useful buying purposes. So great is their need for credit that some are paying heavy interest to loan sharks, and this is the banks' fault. Start making loans tomorrow. Let the bank's customers know that the Valley Bank is in the lending business and we'll have recovery!"

Lend they did! President Bimson worked day and night visiting every branch, meeting hundreds of people, making speeches throughout the state, helping people to make loans, and telling the people that the bank wanted to be of service to the community.

"Money is where people are; that's where I want my main banking activity," Mr. Bimson said, and unlike bankers who concentrated on making large loans, he wanted to extend little ones and lots of them!

The fortunes of the bank gradually turned around, and in 1990 the Valley National Bank with more than 200 branches ranked as thirty-eighth largest among the nation's 48,000 commercial banks.

Since lending is such an important part of a bank's business, to whom does the bank lend its money? During a recent year the major categories of loans at the Valley National Bank included agricultural and livestock loans, commercial and industrial loans, loans to mortgage companies, banks, and other financial loans, real estate loans, construction loans, credit card loans, installment loans, and loans to foreign banks. All this took plenty of money, about $9.6 billion in assets!

Keeping track of this money, plus operating all the other activities of the bank, calls for a large organization which offers many job opportunities. Emphasis within the bank and its branches which serve over seventy-five communities throughout Arizona is on customer convenience. Mention of a few of the innovative ways VNB (Valley National Bank) caters to its customers' needs will show you how much more there can be to banking than the regular activities which we have already sketched.

CUSTOMER CONVENIENCE

Suppose you were starting out on a trip at five o'clock in the morning and discovered you had no money! What would you do? The answer is simple if you were in Phoenix. You would go to the nearest ATM. ATM—Automatic Teller Machine—is by now a widespread banking innovation; VNB first installed them in nine of its Tucson branch offices. Customers welcomed the opportunity to bank their deposits in a machine and cash checks the same way—automatically, without a teller. In fact they were so enthusiastic about the machines that shortly after they were installed some 2,500 transactions were made each day. The machines were spread about the branch offices in such a way that no customer would have to drive more than ten minutes to find an ATM. Obviously, the bank was concerned about how its tellers would regard this threat to their jobs, but meetings held with the employees showed that they did not feel menaced by the machines. Instead they looked upon them as another way that the bank could serve its customers. The tellers did feel, however, that the machines could never do for a customer what they themselves could do.

As part of its public relations and selling program, the VNB Newcomer Service was established to identify and assist newcomers moving into the state.

"Valley National Bank's newcomer service is designed to establish contact with the ever-increasing number of new residents, even before they reach Arizona," Virlea Mays, manager of the VNB's Arizona Information Service, told us.

"An important part of our program is the Arizona Information portfolio," she explained. "The portfolio includes a driver's manual; state map; *Arizona Progress,* the bank's monthly economic newsletter; an in-depth brochure on VNB customer service; a street guide for the city to which the person is moving; and information about VNB's Quick Switch, a unique service that allows one to establish a complete banking relationship before arriving in the state. On arriving, the newcomer simply visits the nearest VNB office and finds everything in readiness to use the bank's facilities."

Introduction of the VNB Banking Card proved a landmark in the bank's history. The new card was not a credit card, but a checking and check-guarantee card that made life easier for the holder. Bearing a photograph of the customer on the front, the card enabled the holder to use it for identification when cashing checks and also for use for ATM transactions. Furthermore, the bank promised that checks drawn by the holder would be guaranteed by the bank for up to $100. Another feature was permitting the card to be used with a new form called a VN Banking

Check. This was designed to make shopping faster and easier for the customer. Standing in line at the grocery store, the customer simply presents a card instead of fumbling around for checkbook and a blank check. The cashier fills in the banking check for the amount of the purchase, overprints the card's number on it, and the customer signs it and receives a receipt. The customer does not need to carry cash or checkbook, can shop on impulse, and the store receives a check guaranteed to be good for up to one hundred dollars. Everyone benefits!

Most banks offer their customers one of two nationally recognized credit cards, *Master Card* or *Visa*. VNB offers both, enabling those who desire to have two charge accounts to budget their expenses and keep track of them by using each credit card account for specific purposes. Thus, one might be used for all household spending and the other to pay automobile and gasoline expenses.

Because most people need help making financial decisions and managing their money, the VNB has held financial planning sessions for those interested in the subject. Specialists discussed life planning, money management, and estate planning in seminars held both in Phoenix and other cities.

One of life's most embarrassing moments results from overdrawing one's checking account, and it is nearly always the result of a simple error. To help protect against the possibility of a "bounced" check, VNB offers "Overdraft Protection from Savings." With this new service, checks written for more than the customer's checking account balance are automatically covered by transferring funds from their regular savings account. The same protection is available for the Master Card credit accounts should they be overdrawn. As long as the savings account has enough money to cover an overdrawn checking or credit card account, a customer can make a purchase at any time by check or credit card without having to go to the bank to transfer money from his or her savings account to one of the other accounts.

None of these innovations would have happened if people had not thought of them, which brings us back to banking being people. Employees have made the VNB a success, and there are some 6,000 men and women dedicated to making the banking services convenient for their customers. Summing up the bank's philosophy in its annual report was the statement: "Record *success*, not record size, is the Valley Bank goal."

There are two important banking departments that we have not covered: the corporate and personal trust departments that you will find in most but not all banks. Traveling some 2,000 miles east to New York City from Phoenix, we will visit two outstanding banks and see how they carry out these important banking activities.

CORPORATE SERVICES

Before he retired to Florida, Paul Sicari was Senior Vice-President in the Corporate Services Department of J. Henry Schroder Bank and Trust Company. Alert, softspoken, and obviously knowledgeable, he joined the bank after serving in World War II and, because he had less than two years high school education, he was determined to apply himself to the job and someday rise to a top management position. Thanks to hard work, conscientiously applying himself to every job that came his way, and always seeking to reflect the bank's philosophy of achieving client satisfaction, Mr. Sicari was elected an officer in 1964.

The J. Henry Schroder Bank and Trust Company is a prestigious English banking firm that dates back many decades. The American bank was founded in 1929 to furnish basic services to United States corporations. Today Schroder is an international network of financial companies that offers banking, investment management, venture capital, and numerous corporate services on a worldwide basis.

The Corporate Services Department that Sicari managed embraced a wide number of specialized services, and commercial banks need many people to provide these services (see chart). Its operations units, which deal primarily with record keeping and processing securities, are lo-

Commercial Bank Employment and Forecast

Year	*Total number of people employed*	
1960		677,000
1970		1,049,000
1980		1,629,000
2000	high forecast	1,990,000
	medium	1,882,000
	low	1,766,000

Source: Federal Reserve Board, Dept. of Labor, Bureau of Labor Statistics. cited in Sumichrast and Crist, *Opportunities in Financial Careers*, p. 9.

cated in the subcellar of a towering office building overlooking New York Bay at the foot of Manhattan. The Corporate Services Department consists of four divisions:

The Custody Services Division is entrusted with safekeeping securities for individuals, corporations and banks—both here and abroad. Not only does the bank collect dividends and interest and give customers a monthly report on all transactions that took place in their account, but it keeps the customers advised of any important developments that may affect their stocks or bonds and which may require action on their part.

Employee Benefit Trust Services are an important part of Schroder's business because whenever a company establishes a pension plan for its employees, it must find a competent bank to administer the program. Not only are pension funds entrusted to the bank; it may also be responsible for deciding how to invest these large sums of money. This calls for a highly skilled staff of in-house professionals, including economists, research analysts, and accountants, whose goal is to see that the funds are safely invested and, just as important, invested in securities which will increase in value.

The Corporate Trust Service Division performs all the work required by a company when it issues bonds, debentures, or notes. Schroder really becomes the corporation's financial agent, as it makes cash payments and handles all the financial arrangements. Here too a staff of experienced men and women handles many intricate details and makes certain every dollar is accounted for.

The Stock Transfer Division is the largest section of the Corporate Trust Department and the one in which Mr. Sicari was most involved. We met him in the reception area on the tenth floor, shook hands, and he immediately led us to an elevator which dropped us into the working area located in the subcellar.

"Here we perform the stock transfer work for many corporations," he explained. "These companies have issued stock which is bought and sold over-the-counter or on one or more of the nation's stock exchanges. Whenever shares change ownership we must close out the seller's account and open a new one for the purchaser. This is one of our biggest jobs. When I came to work here we used to keep all the records on ledger account cards to which we posted information by means of a mechanical bookkeeping machine and typewriter, but now everything has changed. All our records—in fact most of the accounting for the whole bank—are kept on the computer. Would you like to see the computer room now?"

"Of course." He led us to another section of the floor where we could look through a large window at a huge assortment of imposing cabinets and whirling reels.

"You might say this is the heart of the bank," he said, "because here is where most of the record-keeping is done electronically—the data being stored on magnetic disks and tapes. When information is needed, or when lists must be run, or dividend checks prepared, highly trained operators give instructions to the computer. We call it 'programming' and the electronic apparatus does whatever it's commanded to do."

"How does the information actually get into the computer?"

"Let's return to the stock transfer area and I'll show you," Mr. Sicari responded.

Back in the stock transfer area we saw a number of men and women sitting at desks with video displays, working with small machines that looked like the keyboards of typewriters. Their fingers were expertly pushing the keys just as one uses a typewriter, except that they were transmitting information which immediately updated records or was being stored in the computer for future reference and use.

"The computer can do most of our big jobs, like addressing dividend checks, proxies, or envelopes," Mr. Sicari said. Then he laughed, "It does everything but think, and that's why we must have experienced and well-trained men and women to instruct it."

Feeding information to the computer and giving it instructions are by no means all that is accomplished in this division. We followed Mr. Sicari as he showed us groups of employees working at various tasks. Each job must be planned, discussed with corporate officials, and every detail worked out. This takes time and hard work, and we could see that all the employees were absorbed in what they were doing. The office was surprisingly quiet except for unobtrusive background music which somehow made it difficult to believe we were actually in a bank.

Schroder acts as the transfer and dividend disbursing agent for many large corporations and one of Mr. Sicari's duties was to attend stockholder meetings. Here he was in charge of counting the ballots cast for directors as well as other items of business voted upon at the meetings. When all the ballots were counted he certified the results of the balloting.

"The bank also offers other important services for corporations, acting as a company's agent while performing a number of financial services. In fact, we wear many hats.

"Some of the more important services we provide are to act as depositary for tender offers, conversion agent for savings and loan associations, distribution agent for class action settlements and proxy tabulators for proxy contests for the control of a corporation. Most of this work requires processing voluminous documents and securities with a high degree of speed and accuracy in a relatively short time. Other services we perform are to act as scrip agent, liquidating agent, escrow agent, subscription agent, exchange agent, and . . ." He paused and smiled. "I know these terms sound mysterious, but I only mentioned them to indicate the wide latitude of activities we undertake here. I assure you it's not only challenging and interesting, but it can be lots of fun!"

Intimately acquainted with the workings of this department, Mr. Sicari not only made certain that the work flow was maintained and customer satisfaction always achieved, but he also spent time traveling and talking with prospective customers because it is important that new accounts be lined up. Without growth no business can prosper and this is just as true of banking—a fact of which Mr. Sicari is well aware and which, in part, was responsible for much of his accomplishment and the recognition he has received.

THE TRUST DEPARTMENT

A trust department is almost like a different or separate company operating within a bank. Essentially, it helps corporations and individuals manage their financial affairs. Trust officers, called trustees, are responsible for making decisions for their customers, relieving them of the trouble, work, and worry of managing their finances. Originally most trust departments specialized in handling the estates of wealthy clients, but today—through living trusts—there are many ways that trustees can help people use their money to better advantage while they are alive. Many bank clients are people of moderate income, and the services of most trust departments are no longer restricted to the wealthy. Trust departments, as we shall see, do many things which were unthought of until just recently. In fact, a new dimension in personal trust banking has been instituted by some. One example is the Private Banking Group of New York's Citibank.

A full-page, imaginative, and eye-catching advertisement in the *New York Times* told in chatty language all about the PBD—Private Banking Division—a part of one of the largest banks in the financial capital of the world. In answer to the question "Why a Private Banker?" the advertisement, which was directed at men and women who have an annual income of $100,000 or more, stated:

"You are a larger financial entity than many corporations. And, like a corporation, you need a whole range of financial experts—specialists in such areas as taxation, borrowing, investments, estate planning.

"But, rather than expecting you to seek out each specialist on your own, Private Banking Division gives you your own Private Banker. That's one officer who can call on the specialists you need, who can bring the vast resources and skills of Citibank to bear on your financial affairs.

"This doesn't mean that you'll be getting pat answers from an apparent know-it-all. But it *does* mean that your Private Banker has had experience with your field. You won't waste valuable time explaining patiently the ins-and-outs of your profession.

"Different as they are from each other, the Private Bankers of PBD are all highly trained officers of Citibank. They are the 'general practitioners' of financial planning and management. And they are supported by technical specialists across the entire spectrum of banking, investment, and fiduciary services."

Recalling Mr. Bimson's command to lend, lend, lend, we quote from the PBD's booklet, *A Guide to Services:*

"A loan is not a very complicated idea. A bank provides money, and you promise to return it. Yet between the concept and the reality lies every variation of skill and success.

"If your personal borrowings have approached or exceeded $50,000, you may have found that your present bank is no longer able to serve you with the speed or sophistication you want. You may be dealing with a credit specialist who has neither the vision nor training to be constructive in a broader financial context. Or, you may have been referred to a corporate banker who is uncomfortable with or unable to structure large personal and private interest loans.

"We look at a loan as the opportunity to form a partnership with you, the borrower. The single most important quality we can offer this partnership is creativity. It is our job to structure the means for reaching a specific goal. And because the people we serve are special, our loans are often the kind that demand more than the ordinary solution. . . . We practice the '4 C's' of lending: *Capacity* (Can the borrower manage this loan?); *Capital* (Is the borrower financially strong?); *Conditions* (Is the economic and industry climate favorable?); and above all, *Character.*

"At PBD, character is a critical criterion in our considerations, because we lend to human beings. And people don't usually have audited balance sheets."

Take the matter of investing one's money, and you'll find most individuals need professional advice. Those who entrust their investments to the bank have them supervised by a portfolio manager who reaches decisions strictly on the basis of the needs of individual investors. This work is coordinated and supervised by the Personal Investment Committee, which is responsible for over $3 billion in assets—all of which belong to PBD customers.

Turning to trusts—a useful tool to use when building an overall financial plan—some people think of them as mysterious affairs, and with good reason. They can be complex since they are legal agreements and the law is complex. That is why trusts are drawn up by attorneys who know the law best. The bank's role is to manage professionally each trust according to the instructions of the person who establishes it. For example, you could establish a "living trust" to pay money to a child or a relative for a period of time (usually at least ten years), or you could establish a trust into which life insurance would be paid upon your death. The trustee (Citibank) would manage the funds and pay out income to whomever you choose, freeing them from work or worry while receiving a steady income. You may also create a trust through your will. In such a case no money goes into the trust until after you die, and then the bank carries out your instructions regarding how you want the money managed.

In addition, the bank provides special services to the business owner, the professional (doctor, lawyer, engineer, and so on), and the corporate executive, all of whom may have special requirements regarding the management of their businesses, incomes, and investments. To provide these services calls for an extremely capable, highly trained, and experienced staff of professionals.

If working in a trust department sounds as challenging and fascinating as the Citibank booklet describes it, you obviously must expect to spend several years acquiring the necessary background and experience before you can hope to qualify for such a responsible position. There are few departments, however, which offer more opportunity to be of real service to people while exercising your knowledge and initiative.

We have only touched the surface of commercial banking and the many activities which go on before your eyes as well as behind the scenes. From these few pages you can see how important this business is to every American and why the industry takes advantage of the latest technical developments to improve its service and bring both security and convenience to its customers.

Savings banks are important too, and although they do not offer the wide spectrum of services that commercial banks make available to the public, they present career opportunities which you should consider.

CHAPTER 5

SAVINGS BANKS

AMERICA'S FIRST SAVINGS INSTITUTIONS

The Reverend Henry Duncan of Ruthwell, Scotland organized the first modern savings bank in 1810. His experiment was such a success that other banks were started in Great Britain and pamphlets describing their organization found their way across the Atlantic to the United States. A Philadelphian, Condy Raquet, became interested and helped organize the Philadelphia Saving Fund Society in 1816, its purpose being: "To promote economy and the practice of saving. To receive and to invest small sums saved by industrious persons, in order that they may have the advantages of security and interest."

Massachusetts that same year passed the first law permitting the organization and operation of a mutual savings bank and Boston's Provident Institution for Savings was established.

Although these banks were well patronized, the New York State Legislature refused to charter a different type of bank, which is probably why savings institutions are not called banks in New York. DeWitt Clinton and Thomas Eddy, who were interested in founding a savings bank, decided that they must obtain more information about the advantages of saving money if they hoped to convince the legislature of the need for that type of bank. They sent a questionnaire to the banks that were operating in 1819, and even today the replies are amusing and interesting.

A bank in Baltimore reported that, "We do not take over 500 dollars at any time, from any one person. We have an Irishman, a hardworking stone mason, who has deposited 500 dollars, at three different times. Several free blacks, have, from time to time, deposited 100 dollars, and more. We have several instances of women, who, during the whole summer, deposited a dollar per week."

Perhaps the secretary of the Provident Institution for Savings gave the best reason for operating a savings bank:

"The greatest good is, in affording the humble journeymen, coachmen, chamber-maids, and all kinds of domestic servants, and inferior artisans, who constitute two-thirds of our population, a secure disposal of their little earnings, which would otherwise be squandered, or unwisely lent to petty fraudulent dealers, on a promise of usurious interest, which is frequently disregarded."

The banks grew and increased in number, but today the greatest number is still found in the eastern part of the United States. That is because as people pressed westward they turned to farming, lumbering, and mining. What little cash farmers had went back into the farm. Lumberjacks and miners were an adventurous lot, men who would not be satisfied to put their money in a bank that earned them a small return. When they "struck it rich" they often wanted to do big things with their savings.

However, the workers in the city sought a safe place to accumulate funds to tide them over during periods of unemployment and sickness, or for their old age. Mutual savings banks were available to serve them, whereas in the West, stock savings banks and savings and loan associations sprang up to cater to those who sought safe places for their savings.

MUTUAL SAVINGS BANKS

The term mutual savings bank refers to a savings institution that is owned and operated by the depositors, who are the real owners of the bank. All profits are paid to them in the form of dividends. By 1992 there were approximately 317 such banks with over 2,090 branches in the United States, and the thrift industry (savings banks and savings and loan associations) spread throughout the country. (See chart.)

The Philadelphia Saving Fund Society, the oldest, and its parent bank, Meritor Savings Bank of Philadelphia, is also one of the largest, with more than $5 billion in deposit. Of the one hundred largest mutual savings banks, all are located in the northeastern states (including Delaware, Maryland, and Pennsylvania) except the Washington Mutual Savings Bank of Seattle.

It should be pointed out that in recent years many mutual savings banks became stock savings banks, while some savings and loan associations changed over to become savings banks. The form of organization is relatively unimportant to your career future, though obviously job opportunity is brightest in the larger institutions.

In contrast to the mutual savings banks, many of the 48,000 commercial banks have savings departments that offer the same services as mutual savings banks and pay the same rate of interest. All profits

Thrift Institutions Employment

	Savings Institutions	*Savings Banks*
1965	97,600	27,233
1975	169,700	44,050
1985	361,100	80,600
1987	405,900	80,100
1989	400,200	79,500

Source: *Savings Institution Sourcebook '90,* Savings and Community Bankers of America (U.S. League of Savings Institutions) Washington, DC.

earned by these savings accounts go to the owners of the commercial bank, not to the depositors. In the same way, stockholders of savings banks are the recipients of their profits.

Throughout their history mutual savings banks have performed two basic functions: stimulating and protecting the savings of millions of individuals, and channeling these savings into investments that produce an income. Historically, savings banks have concentrated on helping meet the needs for mortgage money in their local communities. During a recent year, two-thirds of their assets did just that, while the remaining cash was invested in bonds and other securities and, where permitted by state law, in some short-term consumer loans.

You may well ask what difference it makes where you put your money, if savings banks and commercial banks pay the same interest rates. The answer is "none." When you deposit money in a stock savings bank or a commercial bank, the profits that your deposits earn for the bank are set aside in a surplus account or paid to the stockholders. If you deposit your extra cash in a mutual savings bank, your money earns interest for you as well as profits because you are a part owner of the bank. Actually you cannot receive more than the legal interest rate set by many states. However, should the bank be dissolved, as a part owner you would share in the distribution of the assets of the savings bank.

SAVINGS AND LOAN ASSOCIATIONS

Savings and loan associations, also called building and loan associations (and cooperative banks in Massachusetts and Rhode Island), differ from stock or mutual savings banks. When you deposit money in one of these banks you are technically buying shares of the bank's stock and then selling them back to the bank when you wish to withdraw cash. In most federal or state chartered savings and loan associations, shareholders may have to wait 30 to 60 days before they can sell their shares to the bank and receive their money. The reason is that about 90 percent of the funds deposited in these banks is invested in residential mortgages and much less cash is held in reserve than in other banks.

Savings and loan associations vary in size from the small to large, not unlike the mutual savings banks, and they too offer a wide variety of career opportunities. The smallest are sometimes called "Mom and Pop" banks, because they were originally run by families out of private homes and stores.

Although you probably will never seek a job with a part-time Mom and Pop bank, it is worth mentioning these tiny businesses that are found principally in Pennsylvania and New Jersey.

Originating in 1831, the first such part-time savings and loan association was the Oxford Provident, which transacted its business in a Philadelphia tavern and made its original mortgage loan to Comly Rich, a lamplighter who needed $375 to finance the purchase of his home. The Oxford Provident was organized like British building societies, where each member made a monthly deposit and the total of all deposits provided enough money for one member to buy a home each month. The new home owner then continued to make monthly installments until the debt was repaid. When all the members had homes of their own, the association was usually disbanded.

During the 1850s another type of savings association, called serial associations, became popular. In these the members made quarterly, semi-annual, or annual payments and the groups operated very much like the building societies, except that members were accepted who wanted only to save money and not buy homes. This was the beginning of savings and loan associations as they are organized today—even the smallest of them—including the Mom and Pop banks.

The Mom and Pop operations could afford to pay favorable interest rates inasmuch as they used volunteer help, operated from convenient premises such as a firehouse, a local social club, or a store, and paid no insurance. The majority of these savings and loan associations have assets under $1 million dollars and usually lend no more than $ 1 0,000 for maximum periods of fifteen years. Many of their customers are afraid to go to a large bank and feel more comfortable and confident in the informal atmosphere typical of these institutions.

Moving west from the Mom and Pop banks to Cleveland, we find an unusual bank dating back to 1935, when the Women's Federal Savings and Loan Association obtained a federal charter and, with assets of only $85,000, opened its one door for business. The nation was in the midst of its most devastating economic depression, the women had little experience in banking matters, and furthermore, it was an unheard-of idea in those days that women should enter the field of banking as executives!

Nevertheless, the idea worked and during the bank's first year of business its reserves increased five times and its shareholders earned a 3 1/2 percent dividend. The bank kept growing, outgrew its original quarters, took over an entire building for its operations, later expanded and modernized these offices, opened a branch, and year after year watched its assets and number of customers grow. Women's Federal had 11 branches and $800 million in assets in 1992. Women managed all the branches except one, and were well represented in top-level management, as high as senior vice president of savings. Actually it was the women of Cleveland's Westropp family who started the bank, and although there were Westropp males on the staff, it was the women who directed the business. The Women's Federal, however, was legally owned by all of its shareholders. Today this successful bank is proof that women are every bit as capable in the field of finance as men!

Mention should also be made here of the American League of Financial Institutions, Washington, D.C., which was formed in 1948 as a national trade association for African-American lending institutions. In that year there were but twenty-two African-American-owned associations in operation and the League therefore had four objectives: *To promote thrift and home ownership among minority groups; To assist in the organization of new associations; To cooperate with, federal, state, and local agencies administering housing functions, and other associations with the same purposes; To conduct research and direct plans for financing housing and other projects for minority groups in a joint arrangement with banks, insurance companies, and other lending institutions.*

Additional money has been sorely needed by savings institutions to alleviate the severe housing shortage for low and moderate income families in the inner city. Therefore, if members of African-American, Spanish-speaking, Asian-American, and native-American groups can be persuaded to put their savings in minority-controlled savings and loan associations, more funds will be available for home financing in communities where these ethnic groups live. The League maintains a continuing effort to encourage those who are financially able—labor unions, insurance companies, educational institutions, and business firms—to make substantial deposits with member associations. The additional housing production made possible by these deposits also encourages increased employment and business opportunities for inner-city residents. The success of the movement may be judged by the fact that as this book went to press there were forty-nine member institutions, including African-American, Hispanic, and Asian-American savings and loan associations operating in twenty-five states and the District of Columbia.

Many people have the impression that savings bank associations are free of problems because most of their money is invested in mortgages, but this is not the case. The State Savings and Loan Association of Columbus, Ohio, had assets of $480 million during a recent year. Its income from interest payments made by homeowners who had obtained mortgages from the bank was rising at the rate of $50,000 a month. However, the bank was paying depositors interest increasing at the rate of $200,000 a month! State Savings and Loan shared this cash hemorrhage with many of the other savings institutions across the country, and recently it was one major cause of a brief shut-down of the savings and loan institutions in Ohio.

A change in government bank rules was the cause of this imbalance of income and expense. In order to make certain that the savings banks would have plenty of money on hand to lend for home mortgages and thus protect the housing industry, these institutions were permitted to issue six-month certificates, which paid higher interest rates than their regular savings accounts. Many depositors immediately switched money from savings accounts to the better-paying certificates and many new depositors were attracted too. Thus, the banks were paying more and more cash to these new depositors.

What the government had overlooked was the fact that many of the mortgages that the savings banks held were written for twenty, twenty-five, or thirty-year periods at much lower rates of interest. The cash coming in as interest payments from these older mortgages was simply not enough to pay for the higher interest rates the banks now had to pay depositors and still have enough money left over to pay for the cost of running the banks.

One solution was the ARM mortgage (adjustable-rate mortgage) with adjustable interest rates that change from time to time to stay in line with prevailing rates. Perhaps someone like yourself will come up with a better solution one day. At any rate, this indicates the uncertainties as well as the challenges that you will find in banking and further proves that it is never a dull or predictable business.

Savings and loan associations and their sister mutual savings banks have by no means dominated the savings field. Another banking institution, a form of cooperative bank known as a credit union, has become a force to be reckoned with as the number of credit unions continues to grow.

CREDIT UNIONS

Credit unions are over 140 years old! They date back to 1849, when Friedrich Raiffeisen, the mayor of a small German town, set up a credit society to enable some of the residents to avoid usurious interest rates and improve their standard of living. He reasoned that if the citizens pooled their savings in a bank of their own they could use the money to make loans to each other at low rates. If an applicant for a loan were known to be honest, that was sufficient security.

The idea was successful, and before Raiffeisen died in 1888, more than 425 credit unions had been established and the plan spread to other countries. In 1907 Edward A. Filene, the wealthy Boston merchant and philanthropist, was traveling in India and first saw groups similar to credit unions. It was a new idea which appealed to Filene. In fact, he was so impressed by what he learned that as soon as he returned home he went to work organizing credit unions in the United States. Before he had finished his work he spent a million dollars on his project.

Two years after Filene resolved to establish credit unions in his own country, the first American credit union was formed in Manchester, New Hampshire. That same year, as a result of Mr. Filene's persistence, the first credit union law was adopted in his home state of Massachusetts. Since then the movement has spread quickly and today, from whatever angle you examine the movement, it is big business!

By 1992 there were close to 14,000 credit unions serving more than 64 million members with assets of more than \$266 billion! The Credit Union National Association, also known as CUNA, tracks this phenomenal growth. A nonprofit organization headquartered in Madison, Wisconsin, it is the service organization for all the state credit union associations. It not only works to improve the operating methods, techniques, and effectiveness of individual credit unions, but also provides public relations, research, legislative, and development support for the national credit union movement.

If you are wondering what a credit union really is, the answer is simple: A credit union is a group of people who have a common bond and have organized to help each other solve their own financial problems. They may be men and women who work for the same company, belong to the same labor union, or church, or who live in the same community. They agree to save their money in the bank which they own and operate, called a credit union, and to make their collective savings available for low cost loans to all the members. The largest number of credit unions serve employees of companies and government agencies, the next largest group serves associations, with the smallest number opening their doors to all the residents of a community.

One such credit union was organized in Hereford, Texas, where a number of bad "black dusters" had hit that part of the west Texas Panhandle. What was once prosperous farm country the storms had turned into a collection of desolate fields, barns, and fences half covered by great dunes of dirt with nearby homes that appeared abandoned.

Lack of cash or credit plagued many residents and this accounted for the group of men and women who had come to the courthouse on March 11, 1936, to listen to a representative of the Bureau of Federal Credit Unions. Many of these people were on the relief rolls and surviving only because the government was shipping surplus food into this city of 2,500. Neither of the town's two banks had sufficient cash on hand to extend small loans to families who might be able to use the money to support themselves or start a small business and stay off relief.

Mrs. Dyalthia Bradley Benson had organized the meeting of citizens who were eager to learn how they might obtain a federal charter for a credit union. Unfortunately, the latest storm had prevented many from coming and it was not possible for Mrs. Benson to obtain even the seven signatures required for a charter application. However, the county librarian volunteered to find additional signers and within a few days the application was on its way to Washington. Four months later the credit union opened for business with Mrs. Benson serving as its treasurer and one of the directors.

Mrs. Benson's enthusiasm was dampened at first because most people were suspicious of a cooperative venture. The first loan of five dollars financed the purchase of a Boy Scout uniform, the second, for twenty-five dollars, bought cow feed for a farmer. Most of the deposits consisted of nickels, dimes, and quarters and by the end of the first year there were but twenty-two members and total assets of $125.44. Mrs. Benson was not ready to give up, though, and week after week she called on members to collect deposits and made it her business to tell others about the credit union and urge them to join. Gradually the credit union idea became better understood and accepted by the community and the membership began to grow. Today the Hereford Texas Credit Union occupies its own building, is a multi-million dollar business, and has a large staff of employees, a tribute to the vision and perseverance of one woman.

Credit unions are democratic institutions: their members are encouraged to invest their savings regularly and from this accumulated capital loans are made to members for practically any good purpose at low interest rates. After all expenses have been paid and legal reserves set aside, the remaining income of the credit union is returned to the members in the form of dividends which provide a reasonable return for the use of the members' money and encourage further savings.

Many employers have found that a credit union helps their company because it contributes to the financial well-being of its employees. Employers permit a portion of the employee's pay check to be automatically deposited in the credit union at the direction of the individual. This "payroll deduction" provides not only a regular means of saving but also a way of repaying loans.

Most credit union loans are made for worthwhile purposes. These include paying taxes, old bills, and medical expenses, as well as for buying automobiles, appliances, mobile homes, or providing cash for education, weddings, and family emergencies. A few credit unions that have sufficient funds even grant mortgages. The character of the borrower is always the basic security for a credit union loan. It is not uncommon for a credit union to lend as much as $2,500 just on the borrower's signature, and more if the borrower has additional security or has a friend cosign the loan. Most credit unions insure a member's life for the amount of his loan balance so that if he or she dies or becomes permanently disabled the loan balance is paid.

A number of credit unions provide financial counseling as part of their service, thus helping members use their money more wisely.

Everybody's Money, published by CUNA, is a large-circulation consumer magazine. Helpful articles advise members how to make their dollars go further, how to buy wisely, and how to budget their money. They also cover a number of other helpful subjects. Consider the following facts about credit unions:

- The credit union movement was through the 1980s growing at the rate of a million new members each year.
- As credit unions grow in size they need more employees with technical and specialized knowledge.
- There are more than 80,000 full-time and part-time positions in American credit unions.
- Staff turnover plus new positions open up more than 5,000 jobs each year.

The job market in credit unions is wide and varied for people interested in a career in cooperative finance, or for those just interested in a good steady job. Credit unions offer job opportunities to a wide range of educated applicants, ranging from those with a high school diploma to technical/vocational school graduates, to college-educated men and women. Even high school students can find after-school jobs in some credit unions.

Applicants without any prior experience can obtain jobs, but a background in accounting, banking, business, communications, finance, management, or personnel is helpful in securing a position. Men and women who have college degrees in accounting, business, finance, personnel, or management are especially needed.

A recent survey of credit unions shows that entry-level jobs at some credit unions have no minimum job qualifications. Vacancies are filled by the most qualified candidates who apply. However, most do have minimum standards. Uniformly, a high school diploma is the key. With it a person can fill almost any job from receptionist to general manager, but without it, there are few job opportunities. Thus a young man or woman who has a high school education can start at the bottom and work their way up, unimpeded by college degree barriers.

However, a college degree speeds up the advancement process, because a person who has a degree can leap past the lower-level jobs and begin her or his career at the professional or managerial level. Increasingly a college degree is required for management jobs, the preferred degree being one in accounting, followed in order by business, finance, management, and journalism. Although experience may substitute for the degree, it is usually experience coupled with some business education that the employer will be looking for.

Post–high school education is required for certain technical jobs such as data processing. Technical training is a must for a computer operator, programmer, and data processing manager. A college background is helpful for other jobs in the technical-professional area and experience in credit unions or other financial institutions is useful too, This applies in the mid-level supervisory area as well, although these jobs are most often filled by people who progress up through the ranks; for example, from teller to cash supervisor, bookkeeper to chief bookkeeper, or clerk-typist to clerical supervisor.

The bulk of the credit-union jobs are found in the clerical area, where a high school diploma is usually the only requirement. Here business education courses such as bookkeeping, business machine operation, and shorthand are helpful. Some positions require certain skills as in the case of the executive secretary who must take dictation and type sixty words per minute.

Post-high school business college or technical school business courses are a definite plus and prior experience working as a cashier or with the public is helpful. Many credit unions provide on-the-job training for certain jobs such as bookkeeping machine operator or data entry clerk.

People with higher education are naturally favored, and as credit unions become more specialized the trend appears to be toward higher educational requirements to fill more technical jobs.

Most credit unions encourage their employees to continue their education in order to prepare themselves for advancement. Most unions assume all the cost of enrollment, tuition, and incidental items for the educational programs they support, as long as the courses pertain to employees' careers. Some credit unions withhold financing until the successful completion of courses and one institution repays the educational costs only if employees stay employed for a year after completing their courses.

Even if advancement opportunities do not materialize immediately, an employee who has shown educational initiative can receive a favorable evaluation during salary reviews. All credit unions review salaries periodically, some more frequently than others, with individual salary increases being based on performance and the cost of living index. Merit carries the most weight in granting raises, followed closely by the cost of living, but seniority is another factor. Individual salary increases and decisions relating to salary scales are usually made by the board of directors and the manager.

Pay scales are generally based on what other financial institutions and credit unions in their communities pay. In the case of credit unions organized to serve employees of a company, their salary scales may be similar to those paid by the company. Wages for clerical workers in credit unions compare very closely with those paid by banks and industry; management salaries, however, may be slightly lower than those paid by banks and trust companies.

The credit union concept of "people helping people" is in its ninth decade of service in the United States. The movement has not only grown during these years but has met aggressive competition and found itself with new powers and ways to serve. Credit union leaders believe that success and maturity bring obligations and that certain social responsibilities go hand-in-hand with being full-fledged members of the financial community.

Since credit unions are cooperatives, they have always "profited for" rather than "profited from" those they serve. They have traditionally supported consumer causes and interests and they will probably continue to support policies and services that benefit the consumer.

Social responsibility was the theme of CUNA's third annual Governmental Affairs Conference. One of the nation's most pressing concerns was obtaining sufficient money for housing, especially for the average worker and family of moderate means. Credit unions recognized that they could help by supporting low and middle-income housing. In addition, many credit unions wanted to see how they could help meet the financial needs of people in inner-city neighborhoods, as well as assist with urban development.

Since the start of the credit union movement, leaders and members, working as individuals, have been among the most active in their communities. Credit unions have not been identified with their members' efforts but now more and more credit union leaders feel that the credit union must become involved as an organization in the social and political concerns of their communities.

This does not mean, of course, that if you seek a career in a credit union you too must become involved in social responsibility projects. However, it is only fair to point out that many of the people with whom you would be working will be active in striving for community betterment and that it might be to your advantage to join them.

What of the future of credit unions? Many credit unions do not feel that success is measured by increased membership but rather by increased services. A recent survey revealed that 87 percent of credit union members also have savings accounts at other financial institutions. It can be seen that credit unions need to expand their services and sell them at least to their own membership.

Technological advances have enabled customers of commercial and savings banks to enjoy such conveniences as the ability to pay bills from their home by telephone; withdraw funds, make deposits, and transfer money between accounts at many locations day or night; purchase traveler's checks from machines in airports; or make purchases thousands of miles from home with plastic cards. Until recently credit unions could not offer these and many other services, but laws and regulations have been changed and credit unions in many parts of the country are now offering many of the same services. Thus, by offering more and better services to their members, credit unions will continue to work toward their goal of becoming the consumer's primary financial partner.

CREDIT UNION JOB CLASSIFICATIONS

The following classified list of positions will give you an idea of the broad range of job opportunity within the credit union movement.

Management Positions

Treasurer/Manager	Branch manager
Assistant treasurer/ manager	Loan Department manager or Loan supervisor
Office manager	Comptroller
Data processing manager	

Technical-Professional Positions

Public/Member relations officer	Collector or Collection officer
Financial or Loan counselor	Computer operator
Loan interviewer	Programmer

Mid-Level Supervisory Positions

Cash supervisor	Accounting supervisor or
Clerical supervisor	Chief bookkeeper

Clerical Positions

Administrative or executive secretary	Accounting machine operator
Chief teller	Receptionist/Switchboard operator
Teller	Typist or Clerk-typist
Loan processing clerk	Mail/Addressing Clerk

Loan disbursement clerk	General office employee
Bookkeeper	(Computer) Data entry clerk
Accounting clerk	

Mutual savings banks, savings and loan associations, credit unions— all share a common purpose of providing a safe place for people to save their money as well as a reservoir of funds for those who need to borrow for any worthwhile purpose. But as we will now see, an aggressive lending policy is a matter of survival not only for these banks but also for financial entities that are not banks in the true meaning of the word. These are really lending institutions that do not obtain their funds from depositors but from other sources. Commonly known as consumer finance companies, they too perform a vital lending service for consumers and job opportunities for you as well!

CHAPTER 6

FINANCE COMPANIES

A NATION OF CONSUMERS

Consumer loans hit an all-time high in the 1980s, according to surveys by *Time, Inc*. They will doubtless reach new heights in the 1990s. Although prices kept rising, people seemed to be buying at an even faster rate as they jammed department stores, specialty shops, shopping centers, discount houses, travel agencies, and real estate offices to buy appliances, clothing, home furnishings, automobiles, luxuries, exotic cruises, and even homes at record high prices. What had happened? Why were Americans storming the marketplace? The answer was simple: Lenders of every kind were fighting to attract deposits from consumers and then to extend loans to those who wanted money.

Mr. and Ms. American Consumer could borrow not only from the commercial and savings banks, the savings and loan associations, and the credit unions, but also from other major lenders—the large finance companies as well as from the "near banks," which included companies like Sears Roebuck, American Express and some stock brokerage firms that were now extending credit to their customers. Consumers had found that prices were climbing faster than their salaries; hence many people were borrowing to purchase not only what they needed, but also things they wanted before prices became even higher. The result of all this mad purchasing was that many people had borrowed beyond their ability to repay. By 1990, total consumer credit had soared to almost $800 billion!

A CREDIT CARD COUPLE

To see how this abundance of credit can lure people into easy spending consider what happened to Eileen and Paul Henshaw, a young couple living in a midwestern city. They had an excellent income: Eileen made $20,000 per year as a fashion buyer for a huge, prestigious department store and Paul earned the same as an insurance salesman. When they married they were jointly in debt for $8,000, of which $4,000 was for a car loan, $500 on charge and credit cards for wedding expenses, $1,000 from a finance company loan for a vacation trip, and a $2,500 personal loan to pay back other loans and medical bills.

Instead of trying to pay off the entire $8,000 debt, Eileen and Paul kept spending and borrowing even more money, which was easy with their ten credit cards and the other credit they could obtain. Although they paid off the $2,500 personal loan and $1,500 on the car loan, they did this by taking a new $5,000 loan to clean up those two loans plus outstanding medical, auto, and department store bills. By the time the baby arrived they owed a total of $9,000 and had bought a home on which they had a $50,000 mortgage. Now they were confronted with extra expenses for the baby and the home. Suddenly they realized that they were hopelessly in debt.

"Whenever we were in trouble, all we did was go get another loan," Mr. Henshaw said. "When I would ask the man for five hundred dollars, he would shove a piece of paper at me and say, 'Here, sign this. You can have a thousand.' Finally we realized it couldn't go on forever, so we talked to a financial counselor who helped us decide what to do. The first thing we did was take a pair of scissors and cut up all those credit cards. Then we budgeted our living expenses and the remaining money to pay off our debts gradually. Finally, we resolved that hereafter we'd save for whatever we needed, and if we didn't have the cash, we wouldn't buy it!"

Thanks to their good sense the Henshaws were not among the more than 200,000 personal bankruptcies filed that same year. Bank credit cards (the best known of which are Master Card and Visa) represent only a small part of all installment credit. In his credit card newsletter, Spencer Nilson stated that: "Never before in the history of our time have there been so many cards, so many lines of credit that exceed people's ability to repay."

BALANCING FINANCIAL OBLIGATIONS

Is this avalanche of credit as bad as it appears? It is true that some families spend beyond their ability to repay, but certainly this is not true of all American families. Many, like the Henshaws, have learned how to avoid the temptation of living beyond their means. What would happen if the government could somehow freeze all credit? It would not be long before the volume of retail sales would drop, the buying of appliances, automobiles, homes and all sorts of luxuries would almost dry up, and as a result stores would close, many factories and other businesses would lay off employees, and the nation's economy would plummet into a depression. More importantly, thousands, if not millions of Americans would be unable to purchase necessities on the installment plan and would have no other way of acquiring them.

"The world seems to revolve around credit," a finance executive told us as we discussed the pros and cons of credit and their effect on careers in this field. "Every time Americans go on a spending spree credit gets a bad name and economists tend to blame it for many of our ills."

"But isn't it true that people overextend themselves? Just consider how many are forced to wipe out their debts by going into personal bankruptcy. It's a solution that helps no one."

He nodded slowly. "True, but haven't we lost our perspective? There are well over two hundred million Americans and the percentage of those who walk away from their obligations by going bankrupt is really negligible." He held up a finger. "But that doesn't excuse them, and we try to avoid lending to such people. That's part of the challenge of this business—keeping bad loans to a minimum. What's wrong, though, with lending to responsible people who want to take a cruise, buy a boat, or a second home?"

Nothing, we said, provided they could afford it.

"Exactly," he agreed, "and this means that they can enjoy these things much sooner than if they had to save up for them. I think you'll have to agree that on balance credit is good for people and for business—provided it's used sensibly. And to help people use it sensibly, it's important and necessary to attract young people seeking interesting and rewarding careers in finance."

We have already touched on the fact that banks must lend, lend, lend, and this brings us to another group of financial companies which offers a multitude of career opportunities because they too must lend aggressively. In fact, lending is their only business!

THE BIRTH OF FINANCE COMPANIES

If you look in the yellow pages of your telephone book under *Financing*, you will find a number of listings that include banks and finance companies. The chances are pretty good that you will find Beneficial Finance Company there because it is among the largest and oldest in the country. Its fascinating history provides a good picture of how finance companies were organized to meet a very specific social and economic need and how such companies have continued to fulfill that need for almost a century.

Whereas today it is very easy to obtain a small personal loan, that was not at all true at the turn of the century. In those days, the low-income worker had no place to go except to the office of a loan shark to request a loan for which he had to pay an exorbitant interest rate. State usury laws set maximum interest rates of 6 percent in the East and up to 10 percent in some western states. However, since these permissible interest rates were too low to cover the cost of making small and risky personal loans, illegal lenders had the business all to themselves. Here the worker who borrowed five dollars for a week was usually charged a dollar interest, or an annual interest rate of 1,000 percent. If the worker wanted to extend the note for a second week, it cost another dollar.

Most of these usurers lent amounts varying from five to fifty dollars, although the average was about twenty. Almost anyone who applied for a loan could get it, but once average wage earners had started borrowing, it became almost impossible for them to repay the loans. Thus, they were trapped. The person who needed a small emergency loan had nowhere else to go except to these illegal sources of money and this abuse had become so widespread that Colonel Clarence Hodson, a successful financier from Maryland, hoped to correct it when he decided to organize the Beneficial Loan Society of Essex County (New Jersey).

BENEFICIAL CORPORATION

"Gentlemen, you have now assumed the duty and privilege of providing small loan service for the workingman.

"Those who need this service number no fewer than thirty-three million adults in this country. They are qualified and entitled to obtain small loans by reason of their industry, character, and credit. Yet there is today no other financial service actually instituted and functioning which meets the need of this great mass of our industrial population. You are investing in an enterprise which will provide a good return with the knowledge that you are cooperating in a good work."

Thus Colonel Hodson welcomed the leading citizens of the area as they dined in Newark's Achtel Stetter Restaurant on the night of February 10, 1914. These professional and business people, ministers, government officials, and private investors had agreed to invest money in the bonds of this new company in order to provide the funds needed to establish a loan service for the public—thanks to the efforts of Colonel Hodson.

Clarence Hodson was born in 1868 in Crisfield, Maryland. After he read law in his father's law office, father and son practiced under the name of Hodson and Hodson. Active in organizing the Bank of Crisfield during 1893, young Clarence became the youngest bank president in the United States. Three years later the governor commissioned him a colonel in the Maryland Militia and for the next four years he served on the military staff and thereafter continued to use his title. During the next several years he extended his financial activities north to Baltimore, Philadelphia, Newark, and then New York City. In 1906 "The House of Clarence Hodson & Co., Inc." was operating as a brokerage firm in Newark, New Jersey, and New York City. That year it organized nine banks, and the following year twenty-three. A tireless worker who thought nothing of staying at his desk until one or two in the morning, Hodson was responsible for starting countless banks, trust and insurance companies, and public utilities in which he served as president or vice president. With his extensive background in finance it was logical that he would see the need for providing small loans.

The year after the Colonel launched the Beneficial Loan Society, New Jersey passed the Egan Act that set a loan limit of $300 with an interest rate of 3 percent per month on unpaid balances, and stipulated that applicants must have character and fitness. This proved a model law for the entire country and signaled the beginning of the end of most of the illegal lenders.

Within a short time the company opened several new offices, and as it did so two patterns of organization were established: First, each new Beneficial office would be a separate corporation organized to sell its securities to local investors but the home office would maintain control by buying a majority of the common stock; Second, each company would have its own board of directors and investors so that they could influence other investors to put money into the company.

Sensing the need for loan agencies to unite and win broad public acceptance, Hodson helped organize the New Jersey Association of Small Loan Brokers in 1915, and a year later seven other state associations were formed. At the same time the American Association of Small Loan Brokers was established in Philadelphia, one of its purposes being to inform the public that lending was a legitimate business, that those engaged in it were honorable, and that enlightened legislation must be adopted to meet the public's needs. It was an uphill battle, for national prejudices against the new industry were strong and the illegal lenders were still entrenched. Also, while on the one hand the public thought interest rates too high, investors thought the rate of earnings was too low.

To proclaim to the world where it stood, each Beneficial office displayed this sign: "Fair and Lawful Charges Only— This Loan Society is a Member of Legal Reform Bureau which offers $100 Reward for Information Leading to the Conviction of any Moneylender Guilty of Making Unlawful Charges." The Legal Reform Bureau was another Hodson creation dedicated to eliminating loan sharks.

Now Beneficial began to grow. From New Jersey it leaped to cities in Pennsylvania, Maryland, and Ohio, and after World War I, further expanded into Virginia, Illinois, and Connecticut. On Beneficial's tenth anniversary it was lending over eleven million dollars and its bulletin proclaimed:

Achievement

Profit-sharing checks for $1\,^1/_2$ percent, paid last month, represent a total return in interest and profit-sharing to original bondholders since 1914 of exactly

100%

Valiantly has The Society fought to aid the small borrower, to recompense its bondholders, to lay its own enduring foundations. In every respect it has achieved success.

Moving on from city to city, representatives of Beneficial were successful in organizing new local societies, but as the company grew so did the problems and the need to keep strict watch over all units to make certain they were operating profitably. Out of this concern came a sound slogan which has guided the company ever since: "Get the money out; Get it back; Keep down expenses." With plans for more than a hundred offices, the Colonel directed that daily reports be sent to national headquarters, that an operations manual be developed for each office to use, and that capable persons be recruited to guide the growing company during the years ahead. Thus the Beneficial Loan Society came of age!

Employees in the New York City headquarters of the Society were encouraged to take night courses and the company paid the cost. The staffs of the various branch offices also needed special training, but in most cities courses were not available to fill the need.

"We will set up a correspondence school, get it accredited, develop our own course of study for office staffs, and also open the service to other finance companies," Hodson declared.

Thus Industrial Lenders Technical Institute Inc., a nonprofit corporation, was organized with a New York State certificate of approval. It was authorized to give correspondence courses in credit standards, collection methods, office procedures, and so on. All the courses ran for two years, ten months each year. Tuition was $4.50 a month and all male loan office employees of Beneficial were required to take the courses.

The Institute not only shared Beneficial's knowledge of the business, but encouraged the adoption of better business methods for the industry, one of them being the concept of making budgeting counsel available to borrowers. After the Institute had been operating for five years it had a total enrollment of 2,600, of which 1,200 students were from Beneficial competitors. Today it continues to operate as Beneficial Management Institute.

By 1927, which was the Colonel's last year at the helm, the 180 offices made over 200,000 loans amounting to over $30 million. Early in 1928 Colonel Hodson was confined to his bed with a heart condition, but he still managed to dictate letters to his secretary. On Friday, January 13, 1928, he had a severe heart attack and died an hour later, just one month short of reaching the age of sixty. Hodson had been a pioneer and now the reins passed to Charles A. Watts, who had already assumed effective command of the operating side of the business. It was not long before he faced his first serious problem.

Four months after Hodson's death the National City Bank of New York announced that it would make loans ranging from $50 to $1,000 to workers at a 6 percent discount rate (actually an 11.58 percent rate) if two people endorsed each loan. Up to this time a few commercial banks had been making personal loans but none of the major banks had shown interest in this business. Most bankers and businessmen felt that personal loans and installment buying were not desirable for the general public. Among them was Henry Ford, who resisted any installment financing until this same year.

President Charles E. Mitchel, in announcing the National City plan, said: "We have now inaugurated a plan for the extension of loan facilities to persons of moderate means who face emergencies which cannot be met out of their current income. Our contacts with people of this class have given us confidence in the integrity and character of the average individual."

"What would be the effect of this announcement by one of the nation's leading banks?" everyone in the personal loan business wondered. Within a short time more than 1,200 banks wrote the National City Bank asking for more information and many of them established personal loan departments. During the first year that National City Bank and its many branches offered the service they made more than 57,000 loans totaling over $16 million. However, when the bank announced that the first year's operation made no profit, the officers at Beneficial Finance and other personal loan companies relaxed, though it was evident that someday banks would move into this field.

Meanwhile another and even more serious threat was occupying Watts' attention. In 1927 Household Finance Corporation had bought up and consolidated into its company the thirty-three offices of the Mackey organization. L.C. Harbison, president of Household Finance, began his cherished idea of reducing interest rates. increasing the volume of business, and hopefully improving his profits. To do this he needed more capital but he had to raise it at a lower cost. In October, 1927, he announced that he was cutting the interest rate charged on loans from $3\frac{1}{2}$ percent to $2\frac{1}{2}$ percent per month, and that he was seeking $7 million of new money by selling preferred stock.

Beneficial was unable to cut its rates because it had to pay more to obtain its capital than Household. Watts, therefore, had no choice but to hold his ground and try to turn it to his advantage. He convinced his associates that it would be best to keep the existing rates and continue to make loans available to the public in amounts under $100, which Household no longer did. Other lending companies followed Watts' lead and a crisis was averted.

"Make no little plans," Charles Watts was fond of saying, and this was never truer than in 1931 when he decided to open no less than twenty-seven branches in the state of California, all during the month of July. Executives, managers, and assistants migrated to the West and the new offices opened on schedule and prospered at a time when the nation's economy was in the throes of the Depression. California had been conquered, but there was still one important state where the company wanted to expand.

Beneficial up to this time had not operated in New York State because the law permitted a rate of only 2 percent per month, giving loan sharks free access to most of the business. Finally, in 1932, a law was adopted permitting a rate which enabled commercial companies like Beneficial to offer their services and realize a profit. Within a year Beneficial opened forty-four offices, realizing Colonel Hodson's dream of doing business in the Empire State.

In 1933 the company not only opened offices in Canada but the *New York Times* announced: "Common stock has been approved for listing by the governing committee of the New York Stock Exchange. This is the first time that the shares of a corporation whose income is derived entirely from the granting of small personal loans have been approved for listing by the Exchange."

Between 1940 and 1941 the company opened an additional fifty-two branches, going into New Mexico, Oklahoma, and Washington for the first time, making a total of twenty-eight states. The other twenty states had either ineffective laws or no laws regulating the loan business, and the problem of illegal lenders in those localities was as acute as when Colonel Hodson first thought of organizing Beneficial. One interesting acquisition Beneficial made was Workingmen's Loan Association in Boston. Established in 1888, it was one of the earliest companies started solely for the purpose of making small loans. Another purchase was the Globe Loan Company of Los Angeles which had eleven branches.

World War II brought a new set of problems. As was the case during the First World War, business fell off because there was a severe shortage of consumer goods—no new automobiles were rolling off the assembly lines—and a large number of wage earners were serving in the armed forces. To boost the company's earnings, Beneficial purchased the Tri-State Transit Company of Louisiana which operated some nine thousand miles of routes in several southern states. This proved a good investment, but Beneficial sold it after the war when a serious strike shut down all operations.

With a good number of its management being drafted into war service the officers asked: "Who will run the branch offices?" The answer was women, and in June 1942, the company selected its first female manager. Since then, an increasing number of women have been assigned management positions with Beneficial.

Following the defeat of the Axis powers, Beneficial resumed its steady growth. A number of noteworthy events took place during the ensuing years, the most important of which are summarized here.

In 1949 Florida passed its Consumer Discount Act which enabled companies like Beneficial to substitute a "dollar cost" for the traditional "percent per month" charge. Now an applicant could see exactly what a loan would cost, as the following table for a one-year $100 loan indicates:

Interest on loan	$ 8.00
Expenses of making loan	2.00
Monthly Service Charge (80¢)	9.60
Total cost	$19.60

At that time, no institution had ever made personal loans for overseas air trips—no one, that is, until 1954 when Beneficial worked out a plan with Pan American World Airways that enabled the airline to sell tickets on credit through Beneficial's facilities. American Airlines soon signed up too, and eventually some thirty-two domestic and foreign airlines were identified with Beneficial's new slogan: "Fly Now—Pay Later."

Beneficial became an international company in December 1959, when it opened its first office at 71 Picadilly Circus, London. More than two dozen additional offices were subsequently opened in the United Kingdom.

Renewing its World War II desire to diversify its operations, Beneficial purchased a large interest in Western Auto, a nationwide chain of stores that sells automotive accessories and equipment.

As the company continued to expand, it outgrew its management headquarters in Newark. Acquiring five and a half acres in Morristown, New Jersey, it erected a four-story brick building of colonial architecture complete with a replica of the historic weathervane on the steeple of Boston's historic Old North Church. In June 1983 Beneficial moved its headquarters with over 1,000 employees from Morristown to a 30-acre all-brick campus-like complex located on a 150-acre site in Peapack, in Somerset County, New Jersey.

Beneficial Center is a total departure from the depersonalized monolithic high rise structures that are the norm for corporate offices. Patterned after early Italian Palladian architecture, Beneficial Center is comprised of six two- and three-story buildings divided into wings. Brick and cobblestone courtyards, formal gardens, arched colonnades, and pedestrian walkways separate the buildings to create the campus-like environment. The central piazza features a stately 88-foot clocktower reminiscent of the campaniles found in many European villages.

Beneficial Center is the headquarters for Beneficial Management Corporation, which supplies management and administrative services to subsidiaries of Beneficial Corporation, including the more than 1,000 consumer credit offices throughout the U.S., United Kingdom, Canada, and Germany. The insurance subsidiaries of Beneficial Corporation are also headquartered here.

In 1971 an "on-line" data processing system, called BENCOM, was placed into operation serving all of the company's branch offices around the world. The cost of operating this system grew, by 1983, to nearly $20 million a year. The computer has automated nearly all of the formerly clerical tasks of running a finance office. It prepares checks, completes loan documents, maintains bank balances, prepares the payroll, insurance claims and prepayment refunds, compiles all office reports, processes a loan payment within five seconds, and completes new loan documents within one minute. The computer center's mail operation sends customer payment books and monthly statements of accounts to Beneficial's customers, amounting to hundreds of thousands of pieces of mail each month.

Beneficial planned to complete installation of its new BENCOM III computer system by early 1993 in more than 900 offices throughout the United States. The company's goal is more efficient customer service through automation and the significant expense of the computer system is evidence of the commitment to achieve it.

There is a Beneficial manager in each of the approximately 1,000 communities in which the company has an office, including more than 900 offices in 41 states. He or she represents the company in the eyes of the customers, the local business community, and the staff. The typical, successful manager is an administrator, credit manager, financial counselor, marketing manager, underwriter, and must be the kind of person who likes people and wants to be helpful to them. As a business person he or she is conscious of efficient operation and of earning a profit in order that investors and lenders will continue to provide the funds necessary in the business.

Should you decide to apply to Beneficial, you will be enrolled in a comprehensive on-the-job training program which is designed to orient you to Beneficial and to develop your proficiency in office functions related to credit, collections, sales, accounting and insurance.

Following this, an employee in a managerial career track will be enrolled in a management development training sequence that includes advanced training in office operation skills, basic managerial functions, and human relation skills. Managerial candidates then must satisfy "acting manager" assignment requirements before being promoted to manager. Completion of this program qualifies individuals to be promoted to manager but advancement does not necessarily stop here! There are opportunities to move up to higher levels of responsibility, to positions such as marketing director, district manager, marketing and training manager, and various staff executive positions in public relations, marketing, advertising, personnel, and so on.

Whether you select the manager training program or an office staff position, the work will be challenging and varied. Most problems you encounter will be human problems, and every problem will be different. In performing your job you will need all the tact you possess, all the imagination you have, as well as all the knowledge of credit and finance you can learn.

In addition to Beneficial, whose address is Peapack, NJ 07977, there are many other consumer finance companies including American, Avco, C.I.T., Household, and Public Finance, to name but a few. To find the names of those companies located in or near your home town, look in the yellow pages of the telephone book under *Finance Companies, Financing,* and *Loans* (they appear under different listings in different parts of the country). Write to the offices of those companies for whom you think you might like to work and inquire about employment openings. Ask if you can make an appointment for an informational interview.

SALES FINANCE COMPANIES

Sales finance companies advance cash to a seller in order to assist individuals in making purchases. Unlike consumer finance companies, which lend you actual cash, members of this industry act as bankers for their customers.

If you purchase an automobile and do not have enough cash to pay for it or elect not to borrow money from a bank or consumer finance company, you can make a down payment and the finance company will agree to give the dealer a check for the balance due. Thereafter you make payments, which include a finance charge, each month to the finance company until you repay the amount it advanced to the dealer. The only difference here is that the sales finance company pays the money directly to the dealer instead of to you as in the case of a consumer finance company. The largest and one of the best known automobile sales finance companies is General Motors Acceptance Corporation. There are also many other similar concerns that can offer career possibilities. If this aspect of the loan business interests you, contact one or more of the companies which are listed below.

Chrysler Financial Corporation, 2777 Franklin Rd., Southfield, MI 48034.

Commercial Credit Company, 300 St. Paul Place, Baltimore, MD 21202.

Ford Motor Credit Company, The American Road, Dearborn, MI 48121.

General Motors Acceptance Corporation, 3044 W. Grand Blvd., Detroit, MI 48202.

Sears Roebuck Acceptance Corporation, 3711 Kennett Pike, Greenville, DE 19807.

Transamerica Financial Corporation, 1150 S. Olive Street, Los Angeles, CA 90015.

You can find the names and addresses of finance companies and their executives that may be located near your home in Dun & Bradstreet's *Million Dollar Directory* or *Standard & Poor's Register of Corporation Directors and Executives*. These books are available in most public, college, or university libraries.

FACTORING

The words *factor* and *factoring* are not in common usage because few people are associated with factors, but this does not minimize their importance. Factoring companies handle billions of dollars worth of business and are a very important part of the financial community.

A modern factoring concern acts for its clients very much as does a banker and a bill collector. Here is how one of these companies that offers factoring service would work for you, assuming that you were the manufacturer of exclusive men's and women's shoes.

As soon as you had shipped an order to a customer, the factor would pay you cash for the goods you shipped. It would then be the factor's responsibility to collect the money from your customer. If unable to do this, it would be the factor's loss, not yours. The advantage of this service is that you immediately have working capital that you can use to manufacture more shoes, and you do not have to wait for your money or go after it. In addition to this service, the factor will also lend you money and provide various advisory services such as management counseling, market surveys, and help in scheduling your production.

By using the services of a factor you do not need a credit department. You receive immediate payment for your sales and this eliminates bad debts, extra accounting expenses, and in addition enables you to use the money productively. Factors charge a flat annual fee plus interest on the money that they may loan to you for rendering these services.

One of the leading factoring concerns is C.I.T. Group Factoring, which merged with Meinhard-Commercial Corporation and William Iselin & Company, Incorporated, the nation's oldest factoring firm. Their combined volume makes C.I.T. the largest organization in the factoring business. It should also be noted that C.I.T. Financial is very active in industrial financing and leasing. All told, it is a large corporation that offers a wide variety of career opportunities in finance. The factoring subsidiary's headquarters office is at 1211 Avenue of the Americas, New York, NY 10036.

We have previously referred to mortgages in connection with the operation of savings banks and savings and loan associations. Because of the importance of mortgages in the field of finance, and the unique job opportunities that mortgage banking offers, it is necessary to explore this aspect of banking in some detail.

CHAPTER 7

MORTGAGE BANKING

Outside San Francisco, workers are erecting a tremendous assembly plant that will soon spew forth an automobile every two minutes, while near Nashville a bulldozer is preparing foundation sites for twenty-two new homes. Meanwhile, in Chicago a steeplejack hoists an American flag above the steel framework of a skyscraper, while down in El Paso a grader levels the ground for a huge parking lot surrounding a new shopping center.

What do these four projects have in common? Simply that they are all activities of the construction business, which amounted to $395 billion in 1990. If you wonder what this has to do with banking, the answer is simple. Each of the projects just mentioned requires financing, and raising the necessary money is the principal business of mortgage banking.

If you have read the previous chapters you will recall that lending money through mortgage loans has been mentioned again and again as an important banking function. The word *mortgage* is not calculated to excite one. The dictionary defines it as a contract covering the pledge of property as security for the repayment of a loan, but please read on, because mortgage banking is one of the most intriguing parts of finance.

Basically, mortgage banking is the science of financing a real estate transaction by providing most of the borrowed money that will make the sale or construction of a building possible. It is the mortgage banker's business to know where to obtain money from out-of-town sources. Thus cash can be provided if you want to buy a home, or assistance can be given local builders of single family homes, apartment houses, condominiums, or commercial and industrial building, so that the money they need to cover their construction costs can be found.

Mortgage bankers are able to do this because they are in touch with important investors throughout the country who have money to lend for building transactions. These investors know they can trust the mortgage bankers' judgment and knowledge of the local real estate markets and that they will invest their funds wisely. Thus mortgage bankers bring money from areas where there is a surplus of funds, usually the major financial centers, into their own communities, where the local banks and saving associations may not have enough extra money to lend.

Mortgage bankers are individuals who specialize in handling mortgages. They may have their own mortgage banking firm, or they may work for a commercial bank, a savings bank, or a savings and loan association. Mortgage banking as discussed in this chapter will revolve around the mortgage banking firm, which is not a bank in the usual sense. But it should be understood that, in general, the functions of mortgage bankers and their staffs also apply to the mortgage department of a bank.

THE MORTGAGE BANKER

Assume for a moment that you are seeking money to buy a restaurant in the downtown area of your city. You have enough money to purchase new tables, chairs, carpets, linens, silverware, and the necessary kitchen equipment, but the only way you can possibly hope to acquire the building is to borrow the money by persuading someone to take a mortgage on the property and give you the money you require as a loan.

You pick up the telephone book, find the name and address of a mortgage banker listed in the yellow pages, and call for an appointment.

After you have explained the purpose of your visit to a loan officer of the firm, you fill out a loan application in which you are to reveal detailed information, mostly about your finances and business experience. As soon as you have completed the form and left the office, various employees will start checking your application. One will verify that what you put down about your past employment was accurate and that your record at each company where you worked was satisfactory. Another employee is checking with your bank to see what kind of a customer you have been: whether you ever overdrew your account, whether you are prompt in repaying loans, and what your average bank balance has been. Meanwhile, a third person is contacting a credit reporting agency where—probably unknown to you—facts are on file about your promptness or delinquency in paying your charge accounts and other obligations. Should your name not be among the thousands for whom information is stored in the computer, the agency will run a confidential check on you and then report back to the mortgage banking firm.

An appraiser will visit the property to see whether it is in a good part of town and judge whether it is a suitable location for a restaurant business. A run-down building next door to the restaurant would probably discourage people from patronizing your business, whereas a row of fashionable stores on either side would be certain to attract patronage. The appraiser will also inspect the building carefully to note any serious defects and later, when preparing the report, will include an assessment of the value of the building and land.

If all of the reports that come to the loan officer's desk are favorable, it will then be determined where to send the application for the mortgage loan. The officer is able to do this because he or she is a member of a nationwide correspondence system that keeps her or him in touch with the major investors from all over the United States. The officer knows the best places to submit applications for single-family residences, for example, but those investors will not be interested in financing a commercial business like yours.

There are a number of investing institutions to which the officer can apply: life insurance companies, commercial banks, mutual savings banks, retirement and pension funds, real estate investment trusts, savings and loan associations, and other mortgage investors, of which the best known is the Federal National Mortgage Association— referred to commonly as "Fannie Mae." Congress established the Federal National Mortgage Association to make another market for mortgages by buying them when usual funds were not available. In 1970 the Association became a "private corporation with a public purpose," and in 1991 it recorded $150 billion dollars in total business volume, giving it the distinction of being the world's largest real estate investor.

Having decided which investor is most likely to act favorably toward the request, the loan officer puts together the application. In your case it might consist of the form you have filled out which includes your financial statement; the appraiser's evaluation, together with a photograph of the building; a summary of the credit reporting agency's findings; and a copy of the sales agreement for your purchase of the building.

Next the application is considered by the lending institution's finance committee. The company probably has certain standards which must be met, and if everything is in order, an officer writes a letter to the mortgage banker indicating that the loan has been approved. Once all the necessary legal documents have been prepared, the mortgage banker advances whatever money is required to close the transaction and then "sells" the mortgage to the investors, in this case an insurance company. The mortgage banker has not yet finished, however. Now undoubtedly he or she will be asked to "service" or manage the loan for the insurance company during the life of the mortgage. The mortgage banker will collect your monthly payments which include what you owe for taxes and insurance. If you should be late meeting an installment, someone in the office will contact you to remind you of your overdue obligation.

If you are unable to meet further payments, the banker will counsel you and try to help you find money to continue your payments, but if this is impossible, it is the banker's job to begin foreclosure proceedings. In other words, the property must be sold so that there will be enough money to repay the investor.

It often happens that after a mortgage banker has arranged for a number of mortgages, they are gathered together in one "package" and sold to an institution as a large block. The banker will then service these mortgages and make certain that the properties are kept in good order. In this way the banker helps the community's economic growth, because he or she can obtain money from other parts of the country—money which few communities may have available to meet the mortgage demands of their own populations.

THE MORTGAGE BANKER'S MANY HATS

The principal challenge of this business is the fact that a mortgage banker must be a specialist in so many areas! Here are the most important functions that you, as a mortgage banker, would have to be ready to perform:

- You must be a salesman—not only to sell your knowledge and experience to people who are seeking a banker to handle their loan for them, but also to investors who are eager to find some sound places where they can invest their funds.
- You must be an appraiser—you need some knowledge of this specialized skill, though you will often rely upon an independent appraiser.
- You should be an able financier—ready to offer complete services to your clients. In the case of a single, one-family home you are merely advising a potential homeowner, but in the case of a large industrial property where financing is needed for construction, you must be able to give advice and handle all details with profession-

alism. As an advisor you must screen potential borrowers and be ready to help if problems arise. At the same time you must know tax laws and real estate regulations because every mortgage banker is involved in these fields.

- You should be a fair negotiator—able to obtain good rates for your clients and at the same time try to assure the highest possible interest rate for the investors.
- You must be a real estate expert—since you are dealing with property transfers you should keep up to date on the latest trends, laws, and developments in this field.
- You must be a good accountant—knowing how to handle and account for the money you receive and then pay over to the investors, at the same time keeping accurate and complete records of all transactions.
- You must be an administrator—whether you are in business for yourself, or head up an organization with twenty-five employees, you must be an efficient executive able to institute accounting and office procedures, train employees, supervise the daily business, and delegate responsibility to others.

Most important of all, you must be alert to new trends and developments in the business and be ready to adjust your own practice to take advantage of opportunities as they come along. The traditional role of the mortgage banker has been to find people who need money and then obtain mortgage loans for them. Today the business has developed into much more than that!

MORTGAGE BANKING TODAY

Diversification is the goal of many mortgage bankers. By adding other lines of business they not only increase their earnings, but also offer more and better services to their clients. This objective enables you to consider various ways you can enter the business too!

Many mortgage bankers started their careers as real estate salespeople. Inasmuch as part of their job when selling property was to help buyers locate financing for their homes, it was logical that some of the real estate agents soon found themselves spending more and more time arranging for mortgages and becoming increasingly knowledgeable about the subject. It was not unusual for a real estate office to find that the mortgage banking part of the business had become more important than selling properties. Thus, if you think you would enjoy working with the public and believe that real estate offers an attractive career, you might become a licensed broker and then gradually shift over into the mortgage banking end of the business. Your experience in the real estate department would prove invaluable for your new position.

Would you believe that many salespeople earn more than the presidents of their firms? Two examples will illustrate what a good salesperson can accomplish. Harvey Brackman, a member of the residential department of his mortgage banking firm, concentrated on finding people who needed mortgage loans to purchase single-family homes. Within 12 months his production totaled more than $8,000,000 in single-family home loans guaranteed by the Federal Housing Administration and the Department of Veterans Affairs. He had been with the firm less than four years when he was appointed branch manager of a six-person office.

Phyllis Temple specialized in the commercial loans department of her firm, and after working hard on a proposed shopping center project, landed her first $2,000,000 loan. She obtained the loan commitment from a life insurance company. The principal tenants of the center were a supermarket, a savings bank, a drugstore, and a department store. A year's work was required to finalize all the details of the leases, as well as the terms of the loan with the insurance investor. Ms. Temple was also responsible for checking from time to time on the construction inasmuch as she was representing the lender. Her ultimate reward—in addition to a large commission—was promotion to the post of assistant vice-president, and this occurred after only three years with the company!

Since many mortgage bankers service a number of the mortgage loans they handle, they have considerable expertise in this end of the business. It qualifies them to provide management for owners of apartment houses, office buildings, industrial parks, and other commercial properties even though they may not have handled the mortgage financing. Good pay and job security are yours if you study for and obtain the designation of Certified Property Manager. It is earned after practical on-the-job experience and formal training.

The mortgage banker may become involved in consumer finance—not the way that Beneficial Finance, C.I.T., or Household are—but by making it possible for home owners to obtain home equity loans. A home is good security for a loan and home owners who cannot obtain loans elsewhere or who have borrowed as much money as any finance company will lend, may find it convenient to borrow against the equity they have built up in their homes. The mortgage banker is the logical person to counsel them and help arrange this financing.

Selling insurance is another activity mortgage bankers have found profitable as well as useful for their clients. Numerous real estate brokers handle fire and casualty insurance because when they sell a home or other property the buyer is usually in the market for insurance coverage. Mortgage bankers have expanded the insurance end of their business, however, and now many offer automotive, compensation, accident, health, life, and other types of coverage. Qualified individuals are always in demand to handle insurance sales, to write the policies, collect premiums, handle claims, and be available for consultation.

In this industry the real estate appraiser enjoys not only top professional recognition but also an excellent salary. With proper experience and training you can obtain an M.A.I. (Member of Appraisal Institute), which is comparable to a C.P.A. in the accounting field. As an appraiser in a mortgage banking firm you would be responsible for handling the firm's property investigations in connection with applications for loans and you might also do independent appraisals for other companies including insurance companies, trust departments of banks, government agencies, and others who lend money and need to have expert reports on the value of buildings and land.

An appraisal is a written statement that sets forth the appraiser's opinion of the value of a particular piece of property at a certain date. The value an appraiser sets on the building and land should be the approximate price estimated in terms of money that a property will bring if exposed for sale in the open market, allowing a reasonable time to find a purchaser who buys with knowledge of all the uses to which it is adapted, and for which it is capable of being used. A strong background in business administration or economics is desirable although not essential for this profession. Some colleges and universities offer courses in real estate and real estate appraising. A number of educational institutions offer appraisal courses sponsored by the American Institute of Real Estate Appraisers.

In old-time movies the role of mortgage collector was played by a man often dressed in a black cape and hat. He twirled his moustache with a wicked sneer as he raised his arm and ordered widows and their children to leave their homes because they could no longer meet the mortgage payments. Today the mortgage collector is usually a trained professional who, instead of being a bad guy, plays the role of counselor and benefactor. Nevertheless, the collector is responsible for performing efficiently, and one of the most important monthly reports the firm issues revolves around her or his work. It is called the "delinquency ratio" and if the ratio is low it is a sign of a well-run department, which is important to investors who do not want to place their money where there is danger that monthly installments on loans will not be paid.

Chester R. Bear, Jr., who was vice-president of Southeast Mortgage Company in Miami, Florida, once wrote in the *Mortgage Banker*: "For the young man or woman looking to a career in mortgage banking, the collection department offers a rare challenge to learn the broad picture of the entire operation. The problems of loan production come to the forefront in the collection section, and a good collector will work with the producer to try to find a solution." At the time Mr. Bear wrote the article the oldest person in the firm was thirty-four years old! "So there is no waiting period," he noted, "just a long, grinding, learning period that never ends, but during which time, we have a lot of fun."

The accountant is as important as the appraiser. Mortgage banking offers opportunity to become involved in the movement of large amounts of money. The usual mortgage company may have from 30 to 50 employees, half of whom are involved in accounting functions of one kind or another. This is because mortgage bankers are involved in handling large sums of money, the smallest company undoubtedly running a minimum of $50,000,000 through its books during a year. In the case of larger companies many times that amount will be recorded in the company's ledgers.

When a loan is initiated it must be recorded, when it is paid off it must be recorded, and all the items that are necessary in connection with buying and selling a piece of property must be recorded. When a mortgage is sold to a mortgage investor a special set of accounts must be established and maintained to keep track of monthly payments, taxes, insurance, special expenditures and fees, and all the other transactions that take place. The number of different types of accounting records that must be maintained is surprising: payroll, income tax, withholding, property taxes, income, expense, and depreciation, to name but a few.

The accounting records are the heart of the business, as in any bank, but the accountant in a mortgage banking firm has more latitude to be innovative than his or her counterpart in a bank. That is because mortgage banking is not regulated as strictly as banks. Furthermore, as we have just seen, the mortgage banker is becoming involved in other activities that can create challenging problems for the accountant. The young person seeking an accounting career who has obtained good training in college and/or business school will find this industry well worth investigating.

Finally, the mortgage banking business offers unusual opportunities for data-processing people as the industry continues to grow in size and complexity. The valuable men and women will be those who understand the business and how it works, perceive its requirements, and anticipate its future needs. If you are trained in data processing and work for a mortgage banker you would be expected to use the technology of data processing to help operate the business efficiently and profitably. To indicate the new horizons that are constantly opening up in this area, consider the matter of records retention— how to find sufficient space to store all the documents that must be kept for years. This problem has given birth to a related activity, COM—computer output microfilm. Instead of having to keep boxes and boxes of reports prepared and printed by the computer, the data in the computer can now be transferred to optical disks, CD-ROMs, microfilm, or microfiche. One small microfiche card can hold the equivalent of 690 pages of computer data. When the card is placed in a reading machine the microscopic print is projected on a screen at a comfortable reading size. This is but one example of the new applications of computer technology which offers a challenging future to those trained in this field.

OPPORTUNITIES FOR WOMEN

What are the opportunities for women in mortgage banking? Let Myrtle Hopkins, who rose to the vice-presidency of the Mason-McDuffie Investment Company in Berkeley, California, show you.

While working for a land development company in the San Francisco Bay Area she became involved in organizing the company's first mortgage department. Her initial responsibilities were of a clerical nature, but this inspired her to learn all she could about the business with the goal of earning advancement. Her interest and dedication were rewarded when, a few years later, she was appointed insurance department manager in loan administration for a large mortgage banking firm. She then attended the MBA's (Mortgage Bankers Association) School of Mortgage Banking and received her certificate of graduation. Later she continued her education, taking courses offered in the local community college, studying the legal aspects of real estate, real estate practices, appraising in real estate, and real estate finance. To complete these courses required many nights attending school as well as evenings of home study, to say nothing of the understanding and enthusiastic support of her husband and family.

Although women are gradually gaining equal opportunity in business, many male executives have been skeptical about women's ability or interest. "In order for a woman to get ahead," Mrs. Hopkins stated, "she must gain the respect and the confidence of her superiors. This can only be achieved through her work performance and her overall knowledge of the business. It has been my experience that patience and perseverance, coupled with an astute knowledge of her trade, can be the most powerful weapon a businesswoman can wield." She summed up the situation by saying: "Many companies are making attractive offers today to entice the well-qualified woman who is unique in her field and considered a specialist in the industry."

The future of mortgage banking looks secure and promising. As long as home ownership is considered good for the country, and the population continues to grow, young people will require homes of their own. Whether they choose single-family or multifamily homes, apartments, or some form of condominium or town house makes no difference, for they will need help with mortgage financing.

However, the problems surrounding the entire mortgage business will become more complex to handle and solve. They call for the services of dedicated men and women who are capable of dealing with whatever difficulties may arise. If you can picture yourself in this situation, you will want to investigate the possibilities that exist for a person of your interests and capabilities.

Finally, a word about the Mortgage Bankers Association of America, which seeks to improve the methods of originating, marketing, and servicing mortgage loans through industry, education, and cooperation with federal regulatory bodies and agencies. Organized in 1914 as the Farm Bankers Association, the MBA now represents some 2,800 member firms—corporations with mortgage companies comprising the largest single group of members. Commercial banks, savings and loan associations, mutual savings banks, life insurance companies, and other organizations whose activities are related to real estate finance are also represented. In addition to the Washington, D.C., headquarters office, there are ninety state and local MBAs across the nation, each of which provides services for its members at the local level.

The MBA sponsors innumerable clinics and seminars and operates the School of Mortgage Banking, which offers three one-week, on-campus, sessions interspersed with two year-long home-study courses. These sessions are offered at different times and in several geographically convenient locations each year. The organization publishes the monthly journal, *Mortgage Banker,* as well as a wide range of other helpful publications covering virtually every phase of mortgage banking and real estate finance. Should you have occasion to contact the Mortgage Bankers Association, its address is 1125 Fifteenth Street N.W., Washington, DC 20005.

CHAPTER 8

THE FEDERAL BANKS

Making things grow is a wonderful occupation thought Rollin Matthews as he stood at the end of the long field of corn and nodded his head with evident satisfaction. The tassels were swaying gently in the breeze and his experienced eye told him that this year he would have a bumper crop, something one did not see in Kansas every year. There was satisfaction and pride in knowing that within a few months the corn he was looking at—his corn—would be distributed somewhere overseas where it would help feed men, women, and children who might otherwise starve. At the same time, he experienced a sense of relief because the sale of these rows of green stalks would bring him the income he needed. Yes, Rollin Matthews was quite aware of the importance of overseas markets for selling his crops, but he knew nothing about how the Export-Import Bank helped make these sales possible.

Meanwhile in southern California, Hazel Atherton concentrated as she bent over her work bench, squinting her right eye to focus on the tiny parts that went into a miniature computer component. She was too busy to think of anything except how to place the almost microscopic screws and wires in their proper places. It never occurred to her to ask what happened to the finished computer—where it went, who purchased it, and what it would do. All she wanted was the opportunity to earn a living doing something that interested her and which provided steady employment. Probably it would have surprised her to know that her job depended first on an American based in some remote foreign country, whose job it was to sell these machines, and second on the decision of the Export-Import Bank to provide money for the transaction.

Mr. Matthews, Ms. Atherton, and millions of other Americans depend on America's ability to sell its products in the export market to overseas countries. Few, however, know that fully one-third of America's farm acreage and one-fifth of its manufacturing jobs depend on the export market. This is because the steady expansion of trade among nations has been one of the driving forces behind the continued economic growth of the United States and other nations. Exports with labels reading "Made in USA" were on the rise during 1992 and this was pleasant news to the officers of the Export-Import Bank, a government agency vitally concerned with encouraging American exports. Exports were not increasing fast enough, however, to solve our crucial balance-of-payments problems, as we shall see later. This is one of the reasons why this bank offers such challenging career opportunities for those interested in world trade.

THE EXPORT-IMPORT BANK

In 1934, when the entire world was gripped in the throes of the depression, Congress first authorized the establishment of an Export-Import Bank to finance trade with Russia. However, until the 1990s the bank had not achieved its original purpose because of disagreement between the two countries over settling the outstanding Russian debts of World War I and the Communist government's policies. Later in the 1930s a second bank was set up to finance trade with all countries except Russia. This was an independent agency of the United States government administered by a five-man board of directors, appointed by the President, whose purpose was to aid in the financing of and to facilitate exports from the United States. At that time the bank's principal goal was to encourage and restore world trade to its former importance.

Then, when World War II engulfed the United States, the bank assisted our allies in the war effort, and following the armistice it contributed some $2 billion for reconstruction. By the 1960s it had become increasingly involved in promoting exports from the United States, often subsidizing shipments of goods from this country by offering easy credit terms to the purchasers. In the case of the developing nations, many of these transactions were in addition to foreign aid programs provided by Congress. To appreciate the urgency and importance of the bank's program during the 1990s, it is necessary to understand the relation between what it does and the nation's balance of payments.

Our nation's balance-of-payments account is a record of all the financial transactions that take place between the United States and the rest of the world. It covers receipts and payments for both private and governmental transactions. A country has a balance-of-payment deficit when it buys more from abroad than it sells. Since 1950, the United States has had a balance-of-payments deficit almost every year, and this has been one of the causes for our steadily rising inflation.

As the cost of imported oil and gas continues to rise to unprecedented levels (up from $3 billion in 1970 to $52 billion in 1989), the balance-of-payments deficit becomes even greater, making the need for increasing American exports more and more critical. If we can sell a larger amount of goods and agricultural products, the additional money received from these sales will offset the dollars paid to the oil-producing nations.

Compared with most government agencies the Export-Import Bank is a very small organization, with only some 400 employees. Nevertheless, the bank plays an important role in supporting American exports of goods and services. This is accomplished through a variety of financing programs to meet the needs of the American exporters, according to the size of the transactions. These programs take the form of direct lending or issuing guarantees and insurance so that exports and commercial banks can help the buyers purchase goods and services without taking undue risks themselves. Ex-Imbank's direct lending program is limited to larger sales of products and services all over the world. Its guarantees and insurance programs have been designed to assist exporters who deal in smaller sales.

The bank may not have at any one time dollar loans, guarantees, and insurance in an amount exceeding $40 billion. The bank can borrow directly from the United States Treasury.

A few examples of how the bank uses its $40 billion to help others purchase United States goods and services will suggest the fascinating work performed in this bank. All of the following financial arrangements were authorized during one month in the 1970s.

Barbados: $3.7 million at 8 and 3/8 percent interest to support the sale of equipment for the expansion and modernization of the Barbados telephone system.

Brazil: $4.7 million at 8 and 1/8 percent interest to support the sale of American goods and services to Deten-Detergentes do Nordeste, S.A., for use in a linear alsylbenzene plant.

Cyprus: $3.8 million at 6 percent interest to support the sale of an earth satellite ground station by ITT Space Communications, Inc. to Cyprus Telecommunications Authority.

Denmark: $13.5 million at 8 and 3/8 percent interest to support the sale of three Boeing 737 jet aircraft to Maersk Air L/S.

Indonesia: $3.2 million at 8 percent interest to support the sale of laboratory equipment by Fisher Scientific Company to the Government of Indonesia.

Philippines: Up to $42.5 million at 8 and 1/2 percent interest to support the sale of American goods and equipment by various suppliers to private and public Philippine firms.

Rumania: $2.4 million at 8 percent interest to support the sale of a polyester industrial yarn plant by Chemtex Fibers, Inc. to Romchim.

United Kingdom: A financial guarantee to cover a $25 million private loan to support the sale of two Boeing 747 jet aircraft to British Airways.

When a foreign country or business wants to buy American services or products, the buyer will often contact other countries such as Brazil, Italy, Germany, or South Korea and ask them to bid also. In most cases there is a government bank or agency that will help finance the purchase of these goods. All this spells competition. As a result, the Export-Import Bank may have to provide better loans in order to make certain that the order is placed in this country.

To decide whether direct aid or a loan will be given, the bank staff studies the "adverse impact" on the United States, although generally the net impact is positive. If the bank's economists find that a large percentage of the items purchased here would be shipped back to the United States and might hurt the American economy, the financing is rejected. The President has lifted restrictions on the bank to allow it to lend to former communist countries, but it may not deal with any nation that has appropriated American property until repayment is made.

"Exports are a major force driving our economy," said John D. Macomber, president and chairman of the Ex-Im Bank in remarks to a congressional committee. "In fact U.S. merchandise exports reached a record level of $394 billion in 1990, growing 8 percent over the 1989 level of $364 billion.

"The Bank is facing up to new challenges in a positive, aggressive manner not only in the emerging markets but in our more traditional and very competitive markets in Europe, Africa, Asia and Latin America," Macomber told a 1991 hearing before the subcommittee on International Finance and Monetary Policy of the U.S. Senate's Committee on Banking.

It is easy to see, therefore, why a career in this bank could bring you great personal satisfaction. As an important member of the government team that is trying to improve the balance of payments, as well as help overseas nations obtain the food, manufactured goods, and various services that they need, your experience, knowledge, and judgment would count heavily in every decision in which you were involved.

Professional staff members required for the detailed reviews of applications for loans, guarantees, and insurance include accountants, financial analysts, economists, engineers in a variety of fields, lawyers specializing in contract law, and computer specialists. Financial analysts and economists compose the largest part of the professional staff.

To evaluate a loan application, a team of staff members, including an economist, financial analyst, engineer, and lawyer, works together. Foreign economic conditions, credit worthiness of the borrower, economic and engineering feasibility of the project, compliance with law and bank policy, as well as other factors are considered. After each member of the team has made an evaluation and drawn up conclusions, the team sends its recommendation to the Board of Directors.

When a guarantee or insurance policy is under consideration, a smaller team or even an individual may work on the application. In such a case the economist or financial analyst is often designated as the loan officer for the project.

Although the headquarters is in Washington, D.C., some international travel is required of most of the professional staff members at one time or another. Frequently, employees are selected to attend national workshops, seminars, and institutes (at bank expense) as part of the staff development program, which assists employees in improving their performance on the job as well as preparing them for additional responsibilities. Employees who attend universities are eligible after one year of employment to receive tuition and other payments for job-related courses.

The Export-Import Bank offers its employees salaries and benefits that are comparable to those of many private banks and financial institutions. Starting salaries for professional staff members depend on education and experience. Salaries are subject to annual review and promotion opportunities are quite good as staff members gain experience and competence. Bonuses or awards for superior performance may also increase one's regular salary.

The bank is a small organization and therefore job opportunities are generally limited and competition is keen. Most positions on the bank's staff require Office of Personnel Management competitive eligibility. They are filled from a federal listing of qualified candidates (WA5-07), open to those with graduate degrees or significant work experience. If the necessary information and forms are not available from your university counselor, write: The Job Information Center, U.S. Office of Personnel Management, 1900 E Street, N.W., Washington, DC 20541.

If you are interested in a career with Ex-Imbank, but don't have a graduate degree or relevant experience, there are some trainee positions open to graduates with majors in finance, accounting, or economics. The bank also employs a small number of students during the year under various intern programs.

For further information write Public Affairs, Export-Import Bank, 811 Vermont Avenue, N.W., Washington, DC 20571.

THE FEDERAL HOME LOAN BANK SYSTEM

The Federal Housing Finance Board is probably not familiar to most readers. However, it regulates nearly all of the institutions in our nation's multibillion dollar savings and loan industry—the country's major source of funds to help finance the construction and purchase of residential housing. In recent years, savings and loan associations have made 30 percent of all mortgage loans for single and multifamily dwellings in the country.

Established by Congress in 1932, when the Depression was nearing its peak, the Federal Home Loan Bank System was given power to regulate and supervise savings and loan associations. This was necessary because, like the regular banks, many savings and loan associations were on the verge of closing their doors. Like the commercial and savings banks, these associations needed a source of funds to have cash on hand when depositors wanted to withdraw large amounts of money. They also needed cash to meet the demands for mortgage funds at times when the public was not depositing enough money to enable these institutions to make loans. The newly created Federal Home Loan Bank System helped the member savings and loan associations to encourage depositors to increase their savings, and it also encouraged the associations to provide mortgage money for families who wanted to buy their own homes. Other members of the system included mutual savings banks and insurance companies.

The law also authorized 12 Federal Home Loan Banks to provide a constant supply of housing funds. Member banks may draw on this financial aid when they need extra funds. In the S&L Crisis of the 1980s, many S&Ls faced insolvency, and the Home Loan Bank System came under severe stress. Congress passed reform legislation that placed the Home Loan Banks under the Federal Housing Finance Board in 1989, when Congress passed the Financial Institution Reform, Recovery, and Enforcement Act.

As the savings institutions were reorganized, Congress also set up the Savings Association Insurance Fund to insure all of the money deposited in savings and loan associations. This insurance company is prepared to reimburse each depositor up to $100,000 should the association where he or she has an account fail. No one to date has lost a penny in an insured savings and loan association. All the taxpayers have shouldered the burden of solving the S&L crisis and strengthening the banking system.

The Federal Housing Finance Board regulates over 2,600 savings and loan institutions, half of which are chartered as federal savings and loan associations, and some as state-chartered savings and loan associations. These institutions are vital to our economy since they hold $709 billion in mortgage loans for 12 million borrowers and $945 billion in savings deposits in 108 million accounts! There were 22,500 savings institutions employing 480,000 people at the beginning of 1990. Though the number of savings institutions is declining, it will remain a significant part of our financial services economy for years to come. They hold 30 percent of all home mortgage loans. It's a fine place to be if you want to be part of America's real estate finance business.

When you consider the importance of the housing industry to our nation's growth—as well as to the needs of every American for decent housing—it is evident that each savings and loan association is a vital part of our economy. The examiners from the Federal Home Loan Bank System fulfill an important role as they ensure that each association operates so that its depositors' funds are always protected and that enough money is made available to meet the mortgage needs of its community.

The Office of Examinations and Supervision is responsible for conducting a periodic examination of each insured savings and loan association. This means that the examiner must go over every phase of the association's operation: the quality of its assets, how great its liabilities have become, how well it is operating, and whether or not it is obeying the various laws and regulations that control it. If the examiners do not know how well an association is carrying out its job, the community in which it does business may suffer.

Imagine for a moment that you are a savings and loan examiner. You will find that each examination represents a new challenge. One trip may take you to a small association in a desolate mining town, the next to a state capital where the association has several branches. Travel is kept to a reasonable amount because you would be stationed where there is a heavy concentration of work. As you work reviewing and checking the books of an association you get a feeling for what is important, what is less so, what should be pursued and what should not, as well as how to go about it in the most efficient way. For example, if you think the only way to judge the quality of a loan that has been made is to look at the property, then you will go out and examine the building. If you find that an association has problems with its management, you may spend as much time talking with the employees as studying the books. You will examine for details, but at the same time sit back and try to visualize the overall operation of the institution.

You will work in a team, the number of men and women working with you varying according to the size of the association and the complexity of its operations. During your first year you may participate in 15 to 20 examinations as a team member, and by the second year you may be in charge of some examinations and be responsible for the final report. The report may contain hundreds of pages, depending on the size of the association, and be accompanied by many times that amount of supporting documents and work sheets, all of which represent two or three weeks of rigorous inspection and critical analysis. The report will be reviewed by a supervisory agent who will then see that appropriate corrective action is taken by the association in line with your recommendations.

The job of the savings and loan examiner is a varied one. You do not just sit behind the same desk all day. There is a constant variation of people, places, and work. Being part financial analyst, part accountant, and part investigator prevents confinement in a narrow specialty. As an examiner you get to know the savings and loan industry upside down, inside out, backwards and forwards.

If you get a college education in accounting, business, economics, statistics, or finance, this may be the ideal career for you. New examiners are put through an intensive course run by agency personnel that is widely recognized for its excellence by state and federal regulatory agencies. Training continues as an essential part of each examiner's career at every stage of development. Courses may range from specialized seminars to university graduate level work for which tuition assistance is available.

Savings and loan examiners usually start at the GS-5 salary level, but some may be hired at the GS-7 level, depending on local job market conditions and college grades. After a year of satisfactory progress, an examiner is normally promoted to the next grade level, and it is not uncommon to be promoted again after the second or third year. Promotions thereafter are generally into supervisory or management positions on a competitive basis, or into other offices of the Federal Home Loan Bank System. It should be noted that the Bank recruits women and minority candidates for examiner positions. To be considered for employment in any of the twelve districts you must take the Professional and Administrative Career Examination (PACE) of the Office of Personnel Management and complete the other application steps specified by the Commission.

If you are not interested in or qualified for the position of savings and loan examiner, but are interested in secretarial, clerical, or other office positions, the Federal Home Loan Bank System could be a good possibility for you too. Inquire at the nearest office. The addresses of the 12 district Federal Home Loan Bank Board offices are listed below.

DISTRICT ONE
  District Director
  Federal Home Loan Bank of
    Boston
  1 Financial Center 20th floor
  Box 906
  Boston, MA 02205-9106

DISTRICT TWO
  District Director
  Federal Home Loan Bank of
    New York
  One World Trade Center
  Floor 103
  New York, NY 10048

DISTRICT THREE
  District Director
  Federal Home Loan Bank of
    Pittsburgh
  One Riverfront Center
  20 Stanwix Street
  Room 300
  Gateway Center
  Pittsburgh, PA 15222-4893

DISTRICT FOUR
  District Director
  Federal Home Loan Bank of
    Atlanta
  1475 Peachtree Street, NE
  Box 105565
  Atlanta, GA 30348

DISTRICT FIVE
District Director
Federal Home Loan Bank of
   Cincinnati
2000 Atrium Two
Box 598
Cincinnati, OH 45201

DISTRICT SIX
District Director
Federal Home Loan Bank of
   Indianapolis
8250 Woodland Crossing Blvd.
Box 60
Indianapolis, IN 46206

DISTRICT SEVEN
District Director
Federal Home Loan Bank of
   Chicago
111 East Wacker Drive
Chicago, IL 60601

DISTRICT EIGHT
District Director
Federal Home Loan Bank of
   Des Moines
907 Walnut Street
Des Moines, IA 50309

DISTRICT NINE
District Director
Federal Home Loan Bank of
   Dallas
5600 N. MacArthur Blvd.
P.O. Box 619026
Dallas, TX 75261-9026

DISTRICT TEN
District Director
Federal Home Loan Bank of
   Topeka
2 Townsite Plaza
120 East Sixth Street
P.O. Box 176
Topeka, KS 66601

DISTRICT ELEVEN
District Director
Federal Home Loan Bank of
   San Francisco
P.O. Box 7948
600 California Street
Room 310
San Francisco, CA 94120

DISTRICT TWELVE
District Director
Federal Home Loan Bank of
   Seattle
1501 4th Ave.
Seattle, WA 98101-1693

FARMERS HOME ADMINISTRATION

Formed in 1935 to make loans to depression-stricken farm families, the Farmers Home Administration now has a much broader purpose. Essentially a United States Department of Agriculture credit agency for farming, it is a far-flung organization that conducts its nationwide programs through nearly 2,000 county and district offices.

As recently as 1960 the Farmers Home Administration (FmHA) was concerned almost entirely with its original purpose of serving as a credit agency for low-income farmers who needed financial aid. Since that time, the Administration has been transformed into a rural development credit agency. Now approximately $6 billion a year flows into rural America, meeting a wide variety of needs that are fundamental to better living in these agricultural areas. In recent years acts of Congress have added large-scale programs that benefit families and communities in every state by providing modern housing, water, sewer systems, and other essential community facilities, as well as helping build up business and industry in rural areas. Recently, Congress created the Rural Development Administration to take over FmHA's programs in rural community development.

Loans and grants that the Farmers Home Administration makes are a supplement to the credit and cash available directly from commercial banks and other lenders in rural areas. In most of its programs, the agency makes loans to qualified applicants who can find no other sources of affordable financing. The grants programs cover a wide range of activities from rural water and waste disposal systems, industrial site development, and farm labor housing to home repair for low-income elderly citizens, and "self-help" home building by low-income families. During fiscal year 1991 the Administration invested $5.75 billion in loans and grants to meet the needs in rural America. Most of this money was lent with the understanding that it would be repaid.

The work of this agency is almost breathtaking! Consider these statistics: In 1989 the FmHA had 614,015 loans on its books to 213,054 borrowers in its farmer programs. The total portfolio of loans hit $27.75

billion by 1990. In a single year 89,119 emergency loans totaling $3.4 billion were made to assist farm operators hit by natural disasters. During another twelve-month period the agency made loans and grants for community business and industry purposes exceeding $2.3 billion. In addition, loans were made to help pay for the construction of 71 hospitals, 37 nursing homes, 22 clinics, and 4 other medical facilities.

The list is almost endless, as Congress has increasingly looked to and used the Farmers Home Administration to help the nation achieve balanced growth. In its own words, "The Congress commits itself to a sound balance between urban and rural people . . . the Congress considers this balance so essential to the peace, prosperity, and welfare of all citizens that the highest priority must be given to the revitalization and development of rural areas." The agency helped farmers weather the farm crisis of 1980–85.

It might be argued that this multipurpose agency has no place in a book on banking careers, but since it makes loans like any commercial or savings bank, savings and loan association, or credit union, it should be mentioned. Furthermore, as can be seen from the number and breadth of its programs, there are career opportunities for almost every kind of skill. You might start out in an office responsible for approving loans for farm residences and transfer to another division where you are involved in making crucial decisions about a large community project such as a health care center or water treatment system. Here you are not just dealing with financial matters, but taking an active part in deciding how the proposed loans and grants will contribute to our nation's economic and social well-being.

If one aspect of banking is making loans, then the most important activity of this agency is a banking function. It has much to offer those individuals who seek challenging positions and want to use their knowledge of finance and economics to aid others. Many other professionally trained men and women may also want to investigate the possibility of a career with the FmHA too. With 1,700 county offices this agency has a tremendous need for secretarial and office personnel of all kinds. Look in your telephone book under *U.S. Government* for the address of the nearest office of the Farmers Home Administration, where you can inquire about employment. If, after earning your undergraduate or graduate degree, a career with the Administration interests you, contact the Assistant Administrator of Human Resources, Farmers Home Administration, Washington, DC 20250.

FARM CREDIT ADMINISTRATION

The Federal Farm Loan Act was passed by Congress in 1916 to establish 12 federal land banks to help farmers who could not obtain credit or mortgages. Commercial banks were not interested at that time in lending to farmers, and therefore set high interest rates and required frequent and costly renewals of those few mortgages that they did take. In addition, many of them would not accept the collateral that most farmers had to offer. At the same time, most of the savings that farmers deposited in their rural banks flowed to urban centers, leaving little money available locally for agricultural needs.

The new law enabled prospective borrowers to form a network of land bank associations from which they could obtain loans. Initially the federal government advanced funds for the new banking system, but gradually the members were able to retire these loans and today all resources of the Farm Credit System are owned by farmers.

In 1923, after a severe depression in farm prices brought heavy losses to farmers, Congress again stepped in and organized 12 federal intermediate credit banks in order to encourage exports of agricultural products. The funds for these banks were raised by selling securities in the metropolitan investment markets. Ten years later, during the Great Depression of the 1930s, the Farm Credit Act was passed, permitting farmers to form a nationwide system of local credit cooperatives offering farmers credit so they would have money to finance their day-to-day operations. These cooperatives became known as production credit associations.

Today the farm credit system consists of 10 Farm Credit Banks. It also encompasses a wide variety of farm credit banks and associations that lend money to rural America with its farmers and ranchers. The Farm Credit Administration is now comprised of 10 Farm Credit Banks; CO-Bank, the National Bank for cooperatives; two regional banks for cooperatives; and about 250 associations.

Headquarters for the 10 credit banks are located in the following cities: Springfield, MA; Baltimore, MD: Columbia, SC; Louisville, KY; St. Paul, MN; Omaha, NE; Wichita, KS; Austin, TX; Sacramento, CA; and Spokane, WA. An intermediate credit bank is in Jackson, MS.

A recent report on the FCA's activities noted that the Farm Credit System is "continuing its slow recovery from the mid-1980s agricultural recession." Though the government is scaling back its administrative hiring, a wide range of job opportunities exists throughout the system and for further information it would be best to consult a local office (check your telephone directory) or write to the Office of Congressional and Public Affairs, 1501 Farm Credit Dr., McLean, VA 22102-5090, or write to the individual bank in which you are interested.

OTHER FEDERAL AGENCIES

No discussion of federal financing activities would be complete without mention of the Department of Housing and Urban Development (HUD). Through its programs in the Federal Housing Administration, it has insured loans for thousands of American homeowners at low rates. Also under HUD supervision is the Government National Mortgage Association, which runs a program that sells mortgage-backed securities to raise more money to fund mortgages. Financial traders call its securities "Ginnie Maes," and the name has stuck to the agency. Ginnie

Mae is part of the money machine behind the American dream of home ownership.

That brings us to look at a hidden force in the real estate lending business—the secondary mortgage market, where bankers buy and sell mortgages from other banks and financial institutions. There may not be too many entry level opportunities here, but if you're interested in aiming for a career here later on, find out more now from a local real estate lender.

Driving this market are two government-sponsored entities: The Federal Home Loan Mortgage Corporation, known to bond traders as Freddie Mac, provides additional funds for housing. It had assets of $335 billion in 1990. Contact the national headquarters or a regional office near you: Federal Home Loan Mortgage Corporation, 1759 Business Center Drive, Reston, VA 22090.

The Federal National Mortgage Corporation, Fannie Mae as it's more familiarly known, also lends to the real estate business. Its assets topped $400 billion in 1990 and Fannie consistently sets records for the biggest financial transactions in the real estate lending markets. Contact its Washington office for more information. FNMA is headquartered at 3900 Wisconsin Avenue, NW, Washington, DC 20016. In addition to the government agencies just described, there are several others that provide special credit or loan services:

- The Rural Electrification Administration helps finance electrical and telephone cooperatives and other organizations that provide utility and telephone service to rural areas.
- The Commodity Credit Corporation provides price supports or establishes minimum prices for major farm products. It also makes loans to farmers who construct storage facilities, and buys and disposes of commodities produced in the United States.
- The Small Business Administration makes loans to small business concerns and aids the small businessperson.
- The Veterans Administration guarantees certain business or farm loans made to veterans.

Study the latest issue of the *United States Government Manual* which lists all of the federal government departments and agencies and explains the duties and responsibilities of each. You may find job ideas there that have never occurred to you. Most employment in the federal government is handled by the United States Office of Personnel Management.

Your own state and local governments may also have jobs of interest to you. Inquire at the personnel office of the administration, bureau, or department where you hope to find employment. For example, state governments hire bank examiners and many have trainee programs for students who have majored in accounting, banking, business administration, or economics. Write the State Banking Department or your State Civil Service Commission at the state capital and request information about training programs and openings for bank examiners.

The government is the nation's largest employer. It may be worth your time to investigate carefully the job opportunities that await you in municipal, county, state, and federal government. Security, good pay, excellent benefits, and equal opportunity are the hallmarks of these employers.

CHAPTER 9

BANKING POSITIONS

Up to this point we have covered the principal areas of banking and touched on the opportunities in each though we have not discussed the jobs themselves in any detail. In this chapter we shall describe typical positions and give you some idea of what each entails.

BANK CLERKS

Most companies need clerks to handle their paperwork, but because of its specialized nature, clerical duties in banking differ from those of most other businesses. In a very small bank one clerk may do many jobs. In larger banks, however, each clerk has a particular assignment and may be given a special title which describes what he or she does.

Bank clerks in some institutions use office machines that are designed especially for use by banks. Clerks called sorters separate various documents such as checks, deposit slips, and other items into different groups and tabulate each batch so that they can be charged to the correct individual accounts. These clerks may also use adding and canceling machines in their work. Proof machine operators use equipment that can sort checks and deposit slips, total their amount, and record all the tabulations.

The largest single group of bank clerks is usually found in the bookkeeping department. Here bookkeeping machine operators may sit at computers, electronic posting machines, or more conventional bookkeeping machines as they record financial transactions. In some banks these employees are known as account clerks, posting machine operators, or recording clerks. The term bookkeeper may be applied to a wide range of job responsibilities: discount bookkeeper, gift or vacation club bookkeeper, trust bookkeeper, interest-accrual bookkeeper, or commodity loan clerk. As part of their work, bookkeeping and accounting clerks may also do routine calculating, typing, and posting. In this group will be found the trust investment clerks who post daily investment transactions of bank customers, and reconcilement clerks who process statements from other banks to aid in auditing accounts.

Banks employ a number of other clerical specialists who perform duties unique to banks. The principal titles include the following: transit clerks who sort checks and drafts from other banks, list and total the amounts involved, and prepare necessary documents to be mailed for collection; country collection clerks who sort the thousands of pieces of mail that come into the bank daily and who determine which items must be held at the main office and which are routed to branch banks for collection; interest clerks who keep records of interest-bearing items that are due to or from the bank; exchange clerks who service foreign deposit accounts and decide the charges for cashing or handling checks drawn against these accounts; and mortgage clerks who type legal papers that deal with real estate transactions on which money has been loaned, and who maintain the necessary records relating to insurance and taxes on each of the properties.

Additional clerical positions are found in electronic data-processing. Electronic reader-sorter operators run electronic check-sorting equipment; check encoders or inscribers operate machines that print information in magnetic ink on the bottom of checks and other documents that are later read by machines; control clerks keep track of the large volumes of documents that flow in and out of the computer department. Other

titles include card-tape converter operator, coding clerk, console operator, data typist, data converting machine operator, data examination
clerk, high-speed printer operator, tape librarian, teletype operator, and
verifier operator.

Banks employ approximately 500,000 clerical workers of whom 20
percent have been bookkeepers; 25 percent secretaries, stenographers
and typists; and almost 20 percent office machine operators. A clerical
position is an excellent way for a high school graduate to start a banking
career.

Most beginning clerical jobs call for a high school diploma, but you
may be given a brief test to determine how rapidly and accurately you
can work, and also whether you can work easily with figures. You need
not be a mathematician but should be able to write legibly and neatly,
be able to do simple arithmetic, and have at least some interest in this
type of work. If you have taken courses in business arithmetic, bookkeeping, office machine operation, and typing, you will have additional
skills to offer which may qualify you for a better starting job.

Some of the beginning or entry positions you may find will include
those of file clerk, transit clerk, keypunch operator, and clerk-typist.
The bank may train you to operate the machines. From your initial
clerical assignment you may earn promotion to teller, credit analyst, or
even to a clerical supervisory post and then to senior supervisor. Even-
tual advancement to an officer position is a possibility if you do an
outstanding job and have taken specialized banking courses to broaden
your knowledge and value to the bank (remember Paul Sicari of Schroder Trust Company?). Your promotions will depend not only on available openings, but also on the way you have performed in each job, your
qualifications for the post, and your motivation. Employment opportunities for bank clerks are good. There were more than 2 million bookkeeping clerks in banks and other businesses; 165,000 billing clerks;
and 33,000 brokerage clerks in 1990, the government estimated. Thousands of openings will arise each year through 2005, according to
government forecasts. This is because banks will expand their services

and open additional branches, and there will continue to be a large turnover among employees thus creating new openings. Although it is expected that as banks make increased use of electronic equipment there will be less demand for various types of clerical workers, these new technologies will not displace large numbers of workers. If your job is taken over by a machine, you will probably be assigned to a new job or to duties related to new banking services.

TYPISTS, STENOGRAPHERS, SECRETARIES

Ability to take shorthand in addition to typing qualifies you for stenographic and secretarial openings that you will find in practically every bank. Most high schools offer typing and other business courses, but if this was not true in your school you can learn how to type in adult education classes, night school, or in a private business school.

Stenographers take dictation, transcribe it, and also perform various typing assignments. Usually a stenographer works for more than one person or may be assigned to a stenographic pool and be called on to work for any one of a number of people. Like typing, shorthand is taught in many high schools, evening classes, and private business schools. You will be expected to take and accurately transcribe 100–120 words per minute.

Secretaries require the same training as stenographers, but they usually work exclusively for one or perhaps two people. In addition to taking and transcribing dictation, they serve as the personal assistants for their supervisors by making appointments, receiving and screening callers, answering the telephone, handling routine matters, and being ready to assist in every possible way. Most secretaries start as stenographers and are then promoted to secretarial positions. In many areas it is possible to take a secretarial course that gives you overall training for the job. This is not essential, however, for you can work your way up to a secretarial assignment or even receive on-the-job training.

BANK TELLERS

Most bank customers have more contact with tellers than with any of the other employees. The man or woman who stands behind the counter or teller window and cashes checks, receives deposits, and handles other transactions for customers is the bank in the eyes of many of the institution's patrons. It is easy to understand, therefore, why tellers are so important in every bank and why it is necessary that you have a personality that is suitable for dealing with the public. A shy individual who would make an excellent clerk might be completely out of place in a teller's position.

As in the case of clerical positions, in the small bank a teller may have many responsibilities whereas in a larger city bank tellers usually are assigned specialized functions; for example, one teller might receive deposits for Christmas club accounts, another sell savings bonds, a third receive and process all payments on customer loans, while others compute interest on savings accounts, sell traveler's checks, or handle foreign currencies.

The most common teller is the commercial teller, who cashes customers' checks and handles deposits and withdrawals from savings and checking accounts. This is a responsible job because of the large amounts of cash handled. If you were employed as a teller, the first things you have to learn before cashing a check would be to ensure that the numerical and written amounts agreed, how to verify the identity of the person receiving the money, and also how to be certain that the account had enough money to cover the check. You would also have to make it a habit to count the cash carefully and when accepting a deposit make sure that the deposit slip was prepared correctly, and that the amount was recorded accurately in the depositor's passbook or on the receipt. You would probably use a computer terminal to record the deposits and withdrawals and also to check on a customer's account balance to see if there was enough money to cover the check.

As a teller, you would report fifteen to thirty minutes before the bank's doors opened at nine o'clock. This would enable you to receive and count the working cash in your drawer, and it would give the head teller time to verify your cash on hand. You would use this money during the day for payments and account for it at the close of business.

As you received cash deposits you would record the amount of each on a slip of paper called a ticket. After your last transaction you would count all your cash, list on a settlement sheet all the deposit tickets you had written during the day, and balance your accounts. You would also sort out the checks and deposit slips and make certain that these agreed. Your first days would be busy ones, but after handling thousands of dollars efficiently and accurately, chances are you would balance to the penny every time.

If this challenging position interests you, ask yourself these questions: Am I neat, tactful, friendly, and courteous at all times? Will I be able to work calmly under the pressure of a long line of customers waiting in front of my position? Will I be patient and understanding with the inevitable difficult customers? Can I work in a small work area at a repetitive job and stand most of the day without undue fatigue? If your honest answers are in the affirmative, and you have graduated from high school, you may qualify for a teller opening at your local bank. For many young people a teller's job is their initial position in the bank. When first employed they usually watch experienced workers for a few days and their training may last from one or two days to two or three weeks or longer. Some banks train their tellers so that they can perform other duties too.

Advancement for tellers is similar to that for clerical personnel. Good job performance, self-improvement, and genuine interest in one's work earn one promotion to head teller or perhaps another more advanced position. If your training and experience are more extensive, however, you might be selected for a manager's position.

Over 515,000 bank tellers serve the public but the number is not expected to increase greatly. The need to replace those who are promoted, retire, die, or stop working for other reasons is expected to create a relatively steady replacement need for this occupation. In time, however, as electronic equipment becomes widely used for banking, the number of tellers will diminish and their job duties will change (see Chapter 10). Demand for part-time tellers will be strong. Full-time tellers may earn from $10,000 to $21,000 a year.

BANK MANAGERS

The difference between the titles of manager, department head, and officer may be great or negligible, depending on the bank and the type of organization it has. In most businesses, a manager is the head of a section of a department, and reports to the department head who supervises several managers. The head of the department, in turn, reports to an officer who is actually an elected official of the bank or company, having been elected or appointed by the board of directors or trustees. A manager might also report directly to an officer rather than to a department head. There are no hard and fast rules in the organization of a bank or the use of titles. As one bank president told us, "I change the organization of the bank and the titles of positions to fit the people and to accomplish what I think makes the most sense." He does not believe in a rigid organization chart or in having to fit people to the various job titles.

After you have worked in a bank for a time, shown your capabilities, demonstrated your sense of honesty, discretion, and loyalty, you will be considered for a promotion to the first step of management, whatever it may be in your bank. You may be selected to serve as head teller, chief clerk, supervisor of a section, or even manager of a department or section. In banks with multiple branches there is need from time to time to select a manager for a branch. This is one of the most interesting positions in a bank because although your title is branch manager, you are almost like the president of your own little bank. It is also a position that is open to more and more women, as illustrated in the case of Pam Webster.

BRANCH MANAGER

"What I like best about my job is meeting people, knowing everyone who comes into the bank," Pam Webster told us, "and feeling that people will ask me for advice and help. That's the advantage of working in a branch instead of the main office."

Pam Webster is manager of the National Bank of Lebanon's Enfield, New Hampshire, branch. Housed in a small, inviting structure, the rectangular banking room has a counter across one side, a private office at the end, and a special drive-up window that any of the tellers can tend. The size of the branch is deceiving because as Ms. Webster explained, the staff can offer every service that is available at the main office except safe deposit vaults.

The NBL (National Bank of Lebanon) covers the city of Lebanon and surrounding area with its seven branches, three of which are managed by women. Lebanon has become a major trading area and growing center for small industrial firms. Since its founding in 1829, the bank has identified closely with the community and been instrumental in the growth of the tri-town area by making capital available for much of the new business. A recent shift from rural to suburban community life and the accompanying expansion of the bank have not changed NBL's interest in helping both individuals and businesses with all their banking and financial needs.

Ms. Webster took a two-year liberal arts course at American University in Washington, D.C. The fall after she completed her studies, she married and moved to West Lebanon, New Hampshire, not far from a newly opened branch of the NBL. That winter Ms. Webster wanted to find a job. "Banking offers good career opportunities," a friend told her, "you can get out and meet as well as work with people." She applied for a position and soon was a teller working behind the counter.

Her banking career was interrupted when her husband was transferred to California. For the next two years Ms. Webster was in the customer service department of the Pacific Telephone Company, obtaining experience that would prove valuable later in her banking career. When the couple returned to New Hampshire the same bank rehired her part-time. Before she could work her way into a full-time position, however, her first child, Jonathan, arrived, followed two years later by Scott. The next ten years were devoted to bringing up the family but when the boys were well into school she became a part-time banker once more, starting again as a teller in the new branch in Enfield.

Three years later she took a full-time post training tellers in the main office. Later, when the bank installed automatic teller machines, she was appointed ATM Coordinator in charge of introducing the machines, showing customers and employees how they worked, and making certain that people knew about them.

"The hardest thing for me is to cope with machines," Ms. Webster confessed. "I'm not mechanically inclined and I'm not a fixer, but I had to learn and I did. You know," she added, "some people are happiest and do their best when working with machines. Others—and that includes me—are what I would call people persons. We have trouble with machines but success in dealing with people."

Doubtless that was one reason why Ms. Webster's next promotion was to customer service work—handling and adjusting complaints, opening new accounts, issuing Treasury bonds, certificates of deposits, and other investment instruments. After a year in this position she was selected to manage the Enfield branch of NBL.

"As manager I'm responsible for the day-to-day operation of this office," Pam said. "This includes supervising the staff, preparing daily reports for the main office, making certain we have adequate cash as well as office supplies on hand, and taking care of the unusual customer problems and requests."

Almost as important is Ms. Webster's desire to find new customers for the bank, as well as prospective borrowers. New business comes as a result of the bank's constant advertising, word of mouth, and the fact that Ms. Webster follows up personally on any leads that may develop.

"One problem we have," she explained, "is that many people are not aware we can do everything at our branch that can be done in the main office. We can make loans, sell traveler's checks, open Christmas club accounts, make advances against credit cards, issue various types of investments, and approve personal and commercial loans."

"Speaking of loans, isn't handling loan requests one of the most difficult parts of your job?" we asked. "Does this bother you?"

She laughed and shook her head. "Not at all, I enjoy it; and remember, it's meeting people, judging, and helping them. Once you run a credit check on an individual and have talked with her or him, you should have a good idea of whether or not the person is a good risk. I find great satisfaction in knowing I've been able to help someone—I'm a people person, remember! Lots of men and women need a little financial boost now and then."

We overheard one customer remark to another, "I just love to bank here, it's so friendly." Undoubtedly this is due to the warmth and cordiality of Pam Webster's staff. Because of the branch's size, everyone seems to have that extra important moment for a special smile and friendly comment or concerned question.

Pam Webster normally works from eight-thirty a.m. to five p.m. except on Fridays when she works until six p.m. Although the drive-up window opens at 8:30 a.m. and the banking floor at 9:00, she is usually at her desk at eight-thirty. One Saturday a month she is in charge of the busy nearby West Lebanon Plaza branch.

Pam shares homemaking activities with her husband, participates professionally as a member of the Financial Women International, sings in a choir, engages in community activities, and volunteers at her sons' school. Thus Pam Webster has not only a successful career as a bank officer, but also a well-rounded and diversified lifestyle as an individual!

BANK OFFICERS

In most banks, the president is responsible for directing the overall operations of the business. In addition, there are one or more vice-presidents in charge of bank departments and a comptroller or cashier who is responsible for all the bank property but who does not actually handle cash. Many of the larger banks have treasurers as well as senior or junior officers who supervise various sections within departments.

The bank officers make decisions in accordance with rules set by the board of directors as well as the state and federal laws and regulations pertaining to banks. They must have considerable banking experience and a broad knowledge of business activities that relate to the operation of their departments. Loan officers consider the credit and collateral of the individuals and businesses that are applying for loans. Trust officers, on the other hand, must understand each customer account before they invest money to support families, send young men and women to college, or pay retirement pensions. Those bank officers who are in trust management must know financial planning and investment. Operations officers plan, coordinate, and control the work flow of the bank and strive for administrative efficiency. A correspondent bank officer is responsible for all the bank's relations with other banks; an international officer, for advising customers on financial dealings abroad; a branch officer, for all the functions of a large branch office. Bank officers are also assigned to auditing, economics, operations research, personnel administration, and public relations.

In many banks, management trainees are groomed for officer and top management positions, but occasionally outstanding employees without such grooming are elected to officer positions. Management trainees are usually selected from those employees who have had college training. An excellent preparation for officer trainee positions is a business administration major in finance or a liberal arts curriculum that includes accounting, economics, commercial law, political science, and statistics. If you have a Master's of Business Administration (MBA) in addition to a social science Bachelor's degree, you have ideal banking qualifications. However, this is not necessary and banks even hire people who have such unusual backgrounds as forestry, chemical engineering, or even nuclear physics in order to deal with the needs of complex, high technology industries with whom they do business.

If you are interested in becoming a bank officer, you should be prepared to work hard, learn all you can about the business, and exercise patience and good judgement. You should also have experience, ability, and leadership qualities to qualify. Promotion may come slowly in small banks where the number of positions is limited, but in large banks that have special training programs, promotions may occur more quickly to one of the many officer openings. This can be true for women too, although banking has long been considered a male stronghold. An example of this occurred early in January 1979, when Sandra S. Jaffee became the first woman to be elected a senior vice-president of New York's Citibank, joining 53 men who held that same title.

Only 35 years old at the time, Jaffee had graduated from Jackson College (of Tufts University) and did graduate work at New York University. Successively she was a management consultant, worked with the New York City Bureau of the Budget, and was hired as an assistant vice-president of Citibank to be involved in "customer engineering," which meant being in charge of setting up and operating the bank's electronic services for its customers. In 1975 she was named a vice-president of the bank, and became responsible for managing and selling the electronic services that the bank offers its corporate customers for transferring stock and reinvesting dividends, among other things.

When Sandra Jaffee became senior vice-president, the bank had 1,043 vice presidents of whom 55, or 4.5 percent, were women. Of the 1,728 assistant vice-president positions, women bankers held 183, or 10.6 percent—proof that women are beginning to make their mark in the banking profession.

There is no question about the importance of bank officers who direct the overall operations of a bank. There are other almost equally essential employees, however, and they are the men and women responsible for lending the bank's money. In a small bank the president or cashier may act as the loan officer. In a larger bank like the National Bank of Lebanon, the main branch may have a customer loan department that handles requests for personal loans, and a commercial loan department that considers the needs of businessmen for additional capital. In the case of a small branch office, the manager, like Pam Webster, acts as loan officer. On the other hand, a large metropolitan bank will need a number of lending personnel in its loan departments that would probably be headed up by officers.

THE LOAN OFFICER

There is nothing mysterious about the loan officer's job. (We shall use the term loan officer, although it might apply equally to an elected officer or a younger employee who has just started working in the loan department.) Your responsibility is to lend money to individuals and businesses which in your opinion are good risks. One banker said that you must be a "jack-of-all-trades" because your customers will expect you to be well-informed on everything from the stock market to collecting stamps. Many businesspeople will assume that you are familiar with their businesses too. At the same time you must have the ability to look behind the figures in financial statements, be able to analyze what you see, grasp the significance of what may not be there, and then decide whether that person will really have the money to repay the loan on schedule.

Perhaps foremost among the qualifications of a good loan officer is what has been called "an affinity for basic arithmetic." You should like to work with figures, since most of your working life will be involved with numbers. You must also be logical in considering each applicant's request, resisting any temptation to be swayed emotionally. If a man desperate for money to pay for an operation on his wife's eye seeks a loan and is obviously a bad risk, you must resist feeling so sorry for him that you grant the loan. If you have too soft a heart, choose another occupation!

As a successful loan officer you should also have a fertile imagination and the ability to put yourself in the other person's shoes. Everyone who sits opposite you in your office is there because he or she has a problem: a need for cash. In a sense you serve two masters: the customer who approaches you for a loan, and the bank that employs you to lend its money. You must learn when to say yes, and just as important, how to say no in such a manner that the customer understands the fairness of your decision and why the loan cannot be granted. You must be ready to make a firm decision each time a person applies for a loan, and remember that you alone are responsible for your decisions.

Writing in *The Journal of Commercial Bank Lending,* Richard McDonald stated: "The willingness to listen to a proposal and the desire to find a solution to the problem are requirements of a good loan officer. At all times he must be constructive in his approach, and if the proposal is not bankable but has merit, he should endeavor to find other means of financing."

A college degree with a major in economics or a business administration degree provides good training for a loan officer. The high school graduate who has demonstrated ability in other banking positions can also transfer into the loan department. Many banks provide training courses and there are opportunities to prepare for a lending officer assignment through seminars and courses sponsored by the banks in your area.

OTHER JOBS IN BANKS

In most banks there are departments not involved directly with banking operations, but which are nonetheless necessary to keep the organization running smoothly. Depending on its size, each department may have openings for clerical, stenographic, and secretarial personnel in addition to other specialist personnel mentioned below. In small banks one or two people may comprise the entire staff, but in a large institution dozens of employees may be required for each of these departments.

The Personnel Department. Because a bank is first of all people who provide the services, and secondly money, the personnel department is an essential one. It is not only responsible for hiring employees, but also for providing all of the personnel services including indoctrination, training, payroll, job evaluation, employee benefit programs, compensation programs, labor relations and employee relations. Personnel specialists are usually hired for these positions and they are generally college trained.

The Purchasing Department. A large or small bank buys many items ranging from paper clips or ball-point pens to furniture, intricate bookkeeping machines, or even station wagons used to transport important visitors to and from the airport. There may be a number of clerical positions that can lead to supervisory assignments as purchasing agent, buyer, or chief purchasing agent.

Public Relations. Advertising and public relations are often centered in the same office, but many banks delegate responsibility for their advertising programs to an ad agency. Public relations is dealing successfully with people with the emphasis on an activity that is beneficial to the public or that endeavors to gain public goodwill and understanding. Most banks conduct their own public relations programs. Professionals on the public relations staff are graduates of a public relations or a journalism school, or they may have had a broad newspaper background.

Maintenance Department. The people who work in this section are responsible for the continuous operation of all the building services. They must make certain that everything is in order when the doors open at nine o'clock and that they stay that way all through the day! Engineers, custodians, electricians, plumbers, carpenters, and other skilled mechanics may be required for the work force.

Mention should also be made of the opportunities that exist in many banks for other professionally trained men and women. For example, if you look forward to becoming an engineer, lawyer, librarian, C.P.A., mathematician, economist, or even a doctor (who would be required for the medical department of a large bank), remember that banks may offer you good employment prospects when you are seeking your first job. Obviously, your best prospects will be the large city banking institutions or government agencies.

WORKING FOR UNCLE SAM

From time to time we have mentioned job opportunities with the federal government, the largest employer in the country. This public employer needs every kind of skill to serve the nation, and only 12 percent of all the jobs are in Washington, D.C. Therefore you should have good prospects for finding employment in your area, even though it might not be in your home town.

Most federal jobs are in the competitive services, which means that you are competing with other applicants and must be evaluated by the Office of Personnel Management. This office accepts applications for federal employment based on the number of jobs government agencies estimate they will fill in various locations over a period of time. After you apply, civil service examiners evaluate your application to see if you are qualified for the kind of work you want. If so, your name goes on a list or register with the names of other people who are qualified for the same kinds of jobs. Then, when government hiring officials have vacancies, they ask for the names of those qualified to fill the positions.

Your chances of being hired depend on your qualifications, how fast vacancies are occurring in the area where you want to work, the number of qualified applicants who want the same kind of job, and the salary level you say you will accept. Because government hiring needs vary from time to time and from one area to another, you might be able to apply in one location for a particular kind of job and be unable to apply for the same kind of work in another location. That is why you should check with the Federal Job Information Center in the area where you want to work.

The Office of Personnel Management maintains a network of Federal Job Information Centers across the country which provide local employment information. If there is no Job Information Center listed in your telephone book contact your state Employment Security Office which will be listed under your state listings.

Even if a government agency is already interested in hiring you, you must be on a civil service register and be referred to the agency as being among the most highly qualified applicants for the job. In order to get on the register, contact a Federal Job Information Center to see whether applications are being accepted in your area for the kind of work you want. If you are not sure of the employment you want, job information specialists may be able to suggest a type of work for which your education and experience might qualify you. They can provide the qualifications information and application forms you will need.

Each government job is classified by a grade-level range based on the job's level of responsibility. Salaries correspond to the grades: the higher the grade, the higher the salary. To qualify for most federal jobs you must have an amount of education and/or experience that is specified for the grade level you want. However, for some openings there is no rigid requirement as to the number of years of education or experience. For these, you must show that you have the knowledge, skills, and abilities needed to do the work by providing information to supplement your application. The qualifications sheet for the job you want will give the particular requirements needed.

The usual minimum age at which you can be hired is eighteen; generally only American citizens may apply for and be appointed to jobs in competitive civil service. You must be physically able to perform the duties of positions for which you apply and you must be emotionally and mentally stable.

The Office of Personnel Management issues a number of informative pamphlets covering all aspects of employment with the federal government. For further information write to the nearest Federal Job Information Center or the Office of Personnel Management, Washington, DC 20415.

CHAPTER 10

YOUR CAREER IN BANKING

By now you should have a fair idea of whether or not a banking career is interesting to you. Before deciding definitely, however, you should remember that having the required character traits is extremely important. Consider each of the following questions and see how you answer them:

Am I thoroughly honest?
Am I discreet?
Am I accurate in whatever work I undertake?
Am I able to get along well with others?
Am I willing to work hard?

Unless you can truthfully answer "yes" to each of these questions, you should not consider banking as a career.

Everyone in a bank from the messenger up to the president must be honest in all dealings. Today many people think that honesty is something that individuals can decide for themselves, but either you are honest or you are not. Handling other people's money, stocks, bonds, and various valuables leaves no question about this. The mishandling or misappropriation of a single penny cannot be tolerated. Honesty includes being truthful and discreet. People in banks deal with confidential information related to the personal and business affairs of all their customers. Being discreet means that all banking employees must maintain absolute silence regarding what they may know about their customers' finances.

Banking and accuracy go hand-in-hand, and many people will accept the bank's word without question when they find that their records do not agree with their monthly statement. Bank employees are not infallible, but they must go to every extreme to achieve perfection and each is expected to try for 100 percent accuracy.

In most banks there are few positions where an employee works totally apart from others. Rather, a high degree of cooperation between employees is expected and required, and the smaller the bank the more important it is that all employees work well together as a team.

Having a genuine desire to be of service is an added advantage for anyone in banking. Service is what a bank sells and therefore every employee must keep in mind the importance of doing his or her very best. Whether a clerk is posting a customer account, a teller is cashing a small check, or an officer is advising a wealthy widow, all are rendering services and the way they perform their respective duties contributes to the bank's reputation for efficiency and good customer relations.

OPPORTUNITIES FOR WOMEN

Did you know that more than two-thirds of all bank employees are women? Furthermore, women hold about 40 percent of the officer and manager titles, and in many areas this ratio is higher. As more qualified women enter banking, the number of women moving up the executive ladder is bound to increase. Many banks have Affirmative Action Programs that are tied to federal Equal Opportunity Employment regulations and these programs are helping women reach the goals they have set for themselves.

According to the Financial Women International, these are the banking areas that a woman may want to consider:

- Commercial Banking—Lending to businesses and attracting corporate accounts, the profit center in most banks.
- Consumer Banking—Offering installment and other loans plus checking and savings accounts to individuals and families.
- Trust Administration—Managing financial assets and estates for individuals and various benefit plans for companies.
- Marketing—Promoting and selling a bank's services and its image.
- Operations—The important nuts-and-bolts activities that keep banks running on a day-to-day basis.
- Personnel Administration—Hiring and training employees, setting salaries and extra benefits.

The larger banks also offer positions—often leading to top executive posts—for attorneys, economists, government relations experts, labor relations specialists, C.P.A.'s, and journalists. Many metropolitan banks have international banking divisions that make loans to foreign business ventures and often operate branches in other countries.

The high school graduate can usually enter banking at the clerical or teller levels and in some cases she may attain a responsible supervisory position in middle management. The chances for advancement, however, are much greater for the college graduate.

Ms. Maxine Calhoun, who was an officer of the Victory State Bank of Kansas City, Kansas, offered the following interesting observations: "The young woman who enters the banking field should not consider that she is working temporarily. For example, my own job started as a temporary one, and lasted sixteen years. Women have a reputation for changing jobs often, but this is not always their choice since personal circumstances can make a change necessary. We have learned from experience that education will make permanent for women the positions they are filling. It is important to remember that banking is a long-range, conservative occupation where recognition and advancement are attained less speedily than in other fields."

Before we close this section mention should be made of the Financial Women International (FWI). This is a professional organization dedicated both to accelerating upward career mobility for women in banking and increasing their job satisfaction. Founded in 1921 as the National Association of Bank Women, FWI has considered diversified educational programs as essential in helping its membership achieve advancement. The Association's Educational Foundation sponsors many educational courses and a nationwide program developed by FWI gives women bankers opportunity to earn a baccalaureate degree in management while they continue working. Seminars and workshops on local, regional, and national levels are also available to the membership. FWI issues career guidance information and may be reached at 1910 Woodmont, Ste. 1430, Bethesda, MD 20814.

BANK COMPENSATION

In order to attract employees with above-average ability, banks offer starting salaries which are at least equal to those paid other white-collar employees who are doing comparable work in the same town or city. Applicants with special skills are paid higher salaries in accordance with their previous training and ability. Furthermore, most banks provide more generous employee benefits than do many other businesses.

It would be misleading to state that you cannot make more money in some other industries. Although the wages paid by certain banks could stand improvement, this disadvantage is usually compensated for by the better working conditions, job security, and extra benefits. *The Occupational Outlook Handbook,* 1992-93 Edition, reports that, in 1992, the median annual earnings of full-time bank tellers were $14,200. The lowest 10 percent earned less than $10,000 and the highest 10 percent earned $21,500. The *Handbook* cited the factors of range of responsibility, size of bank, location of bank, experience, and length of service as factors in salary level.

Bank managers and officers earned substantially more, according to the same publication. The median salary of financial managers was $35,800 in 1990. The lowest 10 percent of managers earned $18,300. The top 10 percent of all financial managers earned over $68,000 a year. Salary levels are affected by range of duties, experience, length of service, size and location of bank, as they are at the entry levels. Also salaries vary between different parts of the country in accordance with living costs. Hence, the high salary paid a teller in New York City, for example, would not be found in a small rural bank.

BANK TRAINING PROGRAMS

The banking industry is noted for the emphasis it places on training and continuing education. It is possible to learn on the job after you start working, but you can broaden your knowledge by studying after hours and you will find that your employer will probably encourage and aid you financially in your efforts to further your education.

Much of the banking industry's formal education program is sponsored by the educational institute of the American Banking Association. The ABA, as it is usually referred to, is a service organization headquartered in Washington, D.C. Its purpose is to promote the general welfare and usefulness of banks. Organized in 1875 during a bankers' meeting in Saratoga Springs, New York, most banks in the fifty states and United States territories are represented in its membership.

In 1900 the ABA established the American Institute of Bank Clerks that has greatly expanded its programs since that time and now is called the American Institute of Banking (AIB). In 1984, more than 300,000 bankers registered for its courses and seminars.

The major function of the AIB is continuing education. Some 600 chapters representing 10,000 member banks sponsor educational programs. These provide opportunity for participants to exchange ideas and experiences as well as improve their knowledge and performance. AIB's educational programs range from one-half day seminars to courses lasting a full semester. These educational activities serve four purposes: (1) to teach fundamental skills and principles to new professionals; (2) to prove advanced concepts in technical areas; (3) to explore issues and applications in specialized banking activities; and (4) to solve problems facing bankers.

Besides the educational activities carried on by the AIB, many schools, conferences, and forums are sponsored by state and local banking associations that are usually open to bank employees. Many colleges and business schools also offer evening courses in banking-related subjects.

In addition to the American Institute of Banking there is the Bank Administration Institute with headquarters in Chicago, Illinois. During a recent year some 12,000 bankers participated in 130 courses given by the BAI in thirty-two cities across the country. These were seminars and other programs designed and conducted by bankers and BAI staff specialists. Nearly 500 bankers serve as instructors in these programs each year. The School for Bank Administration is a key element in the Institute's continuing education program. Some 1,200 banker-students are usually enrolled in the school that concentrates on the following areas of study: audit, control, operations, trust operations, and community bank management.

The BAI undertakes research projects, publishes numerous newsletters and bulletins and offers various helpful services to the banking industry. A magazine, *Bank Management,* covers topics of interest to professionals in the field.

ADVANTAGES AND DISADVANTAGES

There are advantages and disadvantages to working in any industry and banking is no exception. First consider the less favorable aspects of a banking career, and/or the strict requirements which must be met.

Banking is still for the most part a conservative business, although every day bankers are surprising the public with their innovations, indicating that they are gradually throwing off traditions.

Advancement may be slower in banking than in other types of work and ability may not be recognized or rewarded as quickly and fully as in some other fields.

Banking is a sedentary occupation. Work is performed indoors and there are few opportunities for travel.

Banking demands a high level of excellence from its employees and cannot tolerate poor job performance or less than absolute honesty.

Finally, consider the positive features which make banking an attractive field.

Banking offers good job security to the conscientious employee.

Banking offers a variety of interesting careers.

Banking offers excellent educational opportunities.

Banking offers prestige to the individual, since banks are generally held in high esteem.

Banking provides good experience which, if necessary, can be transferred to other occupations.

Banking provides good working conditions, liberal vacations, and other employee benefits.

Banking offers a highly satisfactory vocation because it provides opportunity to be of service to others.

WHAT TO DO NEXT

If you have decided that banking is the career for you, what do you do next?

First, you will want to learn as much as you can about the business and the opportunities it may hold for you. Visit the bank where you or your family do business, or go to the nearest banking institution. Ask the receptionist if you may have an appointment with someone in the personnel department to discuss your interest in working in a bank and preparing for such a career.

Ask your school or public librarian to suggest titles of pertinent books that you can borrow. Unfortunately, there are very few books that explain banking for the layperson. Most of the volumes you will find in libraries were written for bankers or are textbooks on banking aimed at the college student.

SUGGESTIONS FOR HIGH SCHOOL STUDENTS

If you are presently in high school and you are intending to find a banking job after graduation, you should consider taking a business preparatory course. At the same time it would be wise to acquire one or more skills that would enable you to type, take shorthand, and operate a computer, calculator, and other business machines. Without some skills you will be forced to accept a beginning job of a very routine clerical nature. However, if you can show the bank's personnel officer or interviewer that you can type, take shorthand, or operate a computer, and if there is an opening for one of these skills, you stand a much better chance of being hired for a more interesting and better-paying position than applicants who have no special abilities to offer.

If you can find temporary work in a bank before you graduate from high school it will be greatly to your advantage. Many banks offer part-time summer employment, and in some large cities certain banks employ high school students daily for two or three hours after school. This is an excellent means of obtaining experience, earning extra money, and best of all, discovering whether or not banking is the career for you.

Be sure to review your educational plans with your faculty advisor, guidance counselor, or principal, to make sure you have planned the best preparation for that job. Your parents may also be of help; remember that they too are interested in your future.

SUGGESTIONS FOR COLLEGE STUDENTS

If you are in college and looking forward to a banking career after graduation, keep in mind that this is one field that needs men and women who have the broadest possible educational background. A former president of the Investment Bankers Association remarked on this point as follows.

> I personally feel that, as preparation for this business, general education in subjects like English, history, and mathematics is so often more valuable than courses in such subjects as money and banking that the former should be more strongly emphasized. It seems to me that special courses should be recommended only if there is time for them after getting a really first-class schooling in fundamentals.

The principle purpose of a liberal arts college course is to help prepare you to lead and enjoy a fuller life—not necessarily to train you for a specific job. Most banks would prefer to consider a young man or woman who has an alert, well-rounded mind than someone who had devoted most of his college courses to a narrow field of study. There is opportunity, as just pointed out, to receive further specialized training through the American Institute of Banking and other educational institutions once you are on the job. An inquiring mind and a broad background will make you a flexible and valuable employee capable of handling many different assignments. This is not to say that a major in business administration or economics is to be avoided if you have a genuine interest in these subjects. Far from it! What we are urging you to avoid is concentration in one field to the exclusion of other subjects that would help broaden your vision, make you a more interesting person, and more capable of exercising good judgment.

Your choice of subjects is something you will naturally discuss with your faculty adviser, and if you are thinking ahead to a possible banking career be sure to mention this fact at your next meeting!

FINDING A JOB

Some banks recruit their personnel by sending representatives to schools and colleges to sign up promising students before graduation. Tell your faculty adviser, guidance counselor, principal, or college personnel officer about your interest in banking so that you can meet any bank interviewers who come to your school or college.

Register with both private employment agencies and your state employment service, and apply for a position at the personnel office of banks in your community. If a job with the government is your goal, follow the suggestions given in the previous chapter.

You will find a number of good books in your school, college, or public library that explain how to go about finding a job, as well as what to do when you start work. It will pay you to read one or two of these guides so that you will avoid making mistakes and have more self-confidence when you talk with prospective employers.

Be careful about your appearance when you go for an interview. Put your best foot forward, be neat and clean; have your hair combed. A woman should wear a dress or simple suit; a man a suit, shirt, necktie. Remember that the interviewer is trying to visualize you in a specific job. If you appear in sloppy attire, your hair unkempt and your hands grimy, the interviewer will have a difficult time picturing you as a prospective employee. On the other hand, avoid overdressing; you are not going to a party and formal attire is not necessary.

The doors to banking careers are open. Prepare yourself, walk in, and accept the challenge of this exciting industry!

CHAPTER 11

THE FUTURE OF BANKING

The world is changing so quickly that it is not really possible to forecast the future of banking with any degree of accuracy, though it is clear that technology is constantly giving birth to new labor-saving machines and devices that alter ways of doing business, while the actual use of cash is diminishing as money is transferred from bank to bank by computer rather than by armored trucks loaded with stacks of bills and bags of coins.

SERVICES OF THE FUTURE

Bank services are changing too. In the old days some banks had huge vaults for storing fur coats; few if any institutions offer this service now. At one time school savings were an important banking activity to teach youngsters savings habits in the classroom; now they are a dim memory. Banks used to mail monthly statements to their customers at the close of business on the last day of the month. This meant that most of the staff had to work half the night to get the statements completed and mailed the next morning. Now banks use cycle billing, which means that some statements are prepared and mailed every few days and this evens out the work. Until recent times banks did not pay interest on checking accounts. With the advent of NOW (notice of withdrawal) accounts and similar arrangements, most banks credit interest to these accounts. For years banks relied on dignified advertising to attract new customers and additional deposits. Today many banks advertise premiums and gifts to entice large deposits.

During your lifetime banking practices are certain to change. Even now a revolution is gradually taking place as more and more banks make it possible to pay bills by telephone or to buy groceries by using a bank card. It will not be long before you will need to carry little if any cash, as your bank card will enable you to pay bills and buy what you wish without cash. Instead of having to carry your checkbook and balance it every time you write a check or make a deposit, you may carry a tiny electronic device that resembles a pocket calculator. Push a button and it will tell you your latest bank balance!

Not only will you be able to pay bills and buy groceries by phone or card, but you will be able to pay your taxes electronically and what is more, your earnings will be deposited to your account—not every two weeks but daily! It will be a cashless, electronic banking society!

What, you may well ask, will all this do to career opportunities in banking? It has been predicted that all of this sophisticated electronic equipment will call for systems engineers, highly trained operations specialists, and specially trained people to be available for customer contacts. Most of the tellers who now stand behind the banking desk will become financial consultants and money-management counselors. They will sit at individual desks in the lobby, each with a small electronic box and television screen. This will enable a counselor to study a customer's bank account and help the individual plan or adjust her or his financial affairs. Although there will ultimately be fewer employees, those who will staff the bank will be more expert in handling and working the complicated systems. For the comparatively few customers who will insist on using checks, new high-speed, automated equipment will handle most of the required sorting, accounting, and bundling of the checks. Since none of this is going to happen tomorrow, do not let this look into the future worry you!

Whereas a hundred years ago the usual bank building was constructed of granite and made impregnable with heavy steel bars at every window, thus creating the impression of safety and security, this image is no longer important. Today most people look on a bank as a place where intricate accounting and transfers of numbers of dollars take place, not a building where huge sums of money are stored. However, there will be a new and serious problem as more and more money is transferred electronically. Whereas your money was indeed safe in the massive granite building, now the money in your account could possibly be stolen by thieves who have the technical knowledge and ability to tamper with the electronic equipment and transfer dollar amounts from your account to theirs. This will call for another group of expert technicians trained as security people to guard against such electronic thievery. Indeed, many electronic security specialists are already at work in the industry.

The fact that most banks will offer identical services should tend to lessen the individual differences between them. In order to give a bank some individual distinction the management will place special emphasis on personalized service. This means that you, the bank employee, will be responsible for making the customer feel that yours is the only bank where he or she can obtain maximum personalized attention.

COMPETITION

Competition between banks will be heightened as banking laws are changed to permit banks to cross state lines. Some states are resisting invasions into their territories by neighboring banking chains, but many feel that it is only a matter of time before large banks will have networks of branch offices and that ultimately a dozen or so giant banks will control the United States banking industry. Already, mergers have changed the face of American banking (see chart, "Biggest Bank and Thrift Mergers of 1991"). Banks

Biggest Bank and Thrift Mergers of 1991

(dollars in millions)

Acquirer/assets	*Acquired/assets*	*Transaction price*
1. NCNB Corp. Charlotte, NC $69,080	C&S Sovran Corp. Atlanta $49,075	$4,457
2. Chemical Banking Corp. New York $74,130	Manufacturers Hanover Corp., New York $61,329	$2,143
3. Wachovia Corp. Winston-Salem, NC $25,613	South Carolina National Columbia, SC $7,100	$797
4. Norwest Corp. Minneapolis $26,770	United Bank of Colorado Denver $2,123	$471
5. Banc One Corp. Columbus, OH $29,706	Four PNC banks Cincinnati $2,123	$231
6. Firstar Corp. Milwaukee $8,534	Banks of Iowa Des Moines $2,481	$219
7. NBD Bancorp Detroit $26,981	FNW Bancorp Elgin, IL $1,337	$208
8. First Maryland/Allied Irish Baltimore	York Bank and Trust Co. York, PA	$130
9. Comerica, Inc. Detroit $14,342	Plaza Commerce Bancorp San Jose, CA $453	$122
10. First Hawaiian, Inc. Honolulu $5,080	First Interstate (Hawaii) Honolulu $761	$119

Source: American Banker Jan.–Feb. 1991 "Merger Boom of 1991 Will test Wisdom of In-Market Marriages" by Gordon Matthews. p. 1 etc.

merge in order to compete better in a world of financial giants. At the same time, foreign banks are seeking a toehold in this country and to what extent they may become an important factor is another concern to officers of American banks.

FEDERAL BANK SYSTEMS

In the federal government the existing bank systems will undoubtedly continue to operate and Congress will probably add another banking system or two as large amounts of money are needed to solve the energy crisis as well as many of our environmental problems. For example, in mid-1979 President Carter proposed the establishment of a federally funded energy bank to lend money to individuals who would install solar devices and other renewable forms of energy in their homes.

NEED FOR SKILLED PEOPLE

One thing is clear: whether or not America becomes a totally cashless society, no matter how fierce competition may become among the banks, and regardless of the degree of electronic banking that is introduced, banks are here to stay. Banks will continue to perform the important services we have described throughout this book, as well as many new services presently undreamed of, and banks will need people. Although there will be greater demands for technically trained men and women, there will still remain equal need for other professionally educated employees, as well as for those with the ever-necessary clerical, stenographic, secretarial, and related office skills.

Part of the future of banking will be in your hands if you choose it for your life's work. You can help shape its destiny as you become part of an exciting, vital, and growing business. Good luck to you!

SOURCES OF ADDITIONAL INFORMATION

ASSOCIATIONS

American Bankers Association, 1120 Connecticut Avenue, N.W., Washington, DC 20036

Bank Administration Institute, One North Franklin St., Chicago, IL 60606

Financial Women International, 7910 Woodmont, Ste. 1430, Bethesda, MD 20814

Mortgage Bankers Association, 1125 Fifteenth Street, N.W., Washington, DC 20005

Savings and Community Bankers of America, 1709 New York Ave. NW, Washington, DC 20006

ADDITIONAL READING

William D. Bradford, *Minority Financial Institutions.* Los Angeles, CA: Center for Afro-American Studies, University of California, 1988.

Rachel S. Epstein, *Investment Banking.* New York: Chelsea House Publishers, 1988.

James L. Pierce, *The Future of Banking*. New Haven, CT: Twentieth Century Fund, 1991.

Emmanuel N. Roussakis, *Commercial Banking in an Era of Deregulation*. 2nd Ed. New York: Praeger Publishers/Greenwood Press, Inc., 1989.

David Spiselman, *A Teenager's Guide to Money, Banking and Finance*. New York: Julian Messner/Simon & Schuster Inc., 1987.*

Michael Sumichrast and Dean Crist, *Opportunities in Financial Careers*. Lincolnwood, IL: VGM Career Horizons, 1991.

Jo Ann Whatley, *Banking and Finance Careers*. New York: Franklin Watts, 1978.*

*written for high school age group.